Today's Virtuous Woman

By
Elaine Jordan

Author's Notes and Acknowledgements

I want to thank the ladies that came to the Bible classes when I presented the lessons in *Today's Virtuous Woman*. Their comments, questions, and insight helped me to develop and refine these lessons. These Christian women have encouraged me throughout my writing with their faithfulness and Bible knowledge. Many drove close to an hour with a carload of ladies to come to my house. How beautiful are their hearts! I also want to thank Norm Webb Sr. who read all the lessons and checked my Bible quotes.

I have used the New King James Version of the Bible for my lesson quotes. I hope you enjoy this translation.

© **Truth Publications, Inc. 2020.** All rights reserved.
No part of this book may be reproduced in any form without prior written permission from the publisher. Printed in the United States of America.

ISBN-10: 1-58427-493-X

ISBN-13: 978-1-58427-493-3

Truth Publications, Inc.
CEI Bookstore
220 S. Marion St., Athens, AL 35611
855-492-6657
sales@truthpublications.com
www.truthbooks.com

Table of Contents

Lessons	Page
1. The Proverbial Woman	5
2. Husband and Wife	17
3. Motherhood and the Household	26
4. Money Management	37
5. Charity and the Community	49
6. Prayer	65
7. Personal Outlook and Our Reputations	71
8. Time Management	89
9. Beauty and Fashion	95
10. Wise Words	106
11. Maturing in Body and Spirit	117
12. The Storms of Life	129
13. Who Fears the Lord	141

The Proverbial Woman

Chapter 1—The Proverbial Woman

What can the virtuous woman in Proverbs 31:10-31 teach us today about being a godly woman?

Presently women wanting godly lives are criticized for living in the past. Or a godly woman looks into the Bible and cannot see herself or see how the Bible is useful today where women are Senators, company presidents, astronauts, police officers, and soldiers.

All of us know the verses of Proverbs 31 describing the virtuous woman, but we are not sure she would live the same way today. Perhaps Coffman's commentary may be one of the best summaries of those verses. "Her many wonderful qualities are thrift, industry, kindness, compassion, efficiency, business sense, discretion, discernment, true love, faithfulness, and all the other graces and virtues of true womanhood. However, her crowning glory is in the concluding verses: 'A woman that feareth Jehovah!'" (Coffman, notes on Prov. 31:10).

Many women today can't see themselves in these verses from Proverbs 31. The virtuous woman worked too hard, her example is too demanding, and she lived a long time ago. Then we say she certainly was an affluent woman with a lot of servants in a different era to complete all those responsibilities. How can we be like her without all her resources? We forget that everything in the Bible is there for our edification. Modern women can learn a lot from this proverbial virtuous woman. We need to look for the lessons.

Today, just like yesterday, all women are different and have different skills and abilities. Some marry, and some stay single. Some have children, and some do not. Some have a lot of education, and some have very little. Some have many talents and resources, and some have only a few. How can we learn from the virtuous woman when we are not like her? Not many of us are equal!

Picking specific lessons from the text to apply in our lives makes it easier to let the virtuous woman help us in our everyday lives. Then her example is not so daunting. When we recognize that she is an ideal, a model, for us to pattern ourselves, we can see that she can help us in our lives. The description of the virtuous woman has several different areas for separate consideration. Let's divide up the verses into some areas to simplify our discussion of her.

- Her marriage and husband
- Her family and household
- Her community and church
- Her qualities
- Her business pursuits
- Her relationship with God

Her Marriage and Husband

The heart of her husband safely trusts her; so he will have no lack of gain. She does him good and not evil all the days of her life (vv. 11-12).

Her husband is known in the gates, when he sits among the elders of the land (v. 23).

The Proverbial Woman

Her children rise up and call her blessed; her husband also, and he praises her: "Many daughters have done well, but you excel them all" (vv. 28-29).

The Proverbial woman's marriage is strong because she has chosen a good husband, and they work together to intertwine their lives. Her husband trusts her, and she does him good and not evil. The community and the family know of their strong bond and reputations. Her husband blesses her in verse 29 because she is part of who he is. She is as valuable to him as he is vital to her.

These verses permit no room for marital infidelity or a lack of commitment for the virtuous woman. I cannot imagine how she would even allow herself in a questionable situation. This woman's priorities are not pop culture, high fashion, or social standing, but her marriage and husband.

The husband trusts the virtuous woman to manage his household and resources well. After all, there was no phone or email with instantaneous guidance from the husband to the wife during the time of these verses. These verses are not about a woman with no authorization for decision making; however, she respected her husband's authority as the family leader. They work together for the good of their family and community, but their marriage is most important of all.

Her Family and Household

She is like the merchant ships, she brings her food from afar. She also rises while it is yet night, and provides food for her household and a portion for her maidservants (vv. 14-15).

She stretches out her hands to the distaff, and her hand holds the spindle (v. 19).

She is not afraid of snow for her household, for all her household is clothed with scarlet (v. 21).

She watches over the ways of her household, and does not eat the bread of idleness. Her children rise up and call her blessed; her husband also, and he praises her (vv. 27-28).

These verses tell us that the virtuous woman is very busy! She provides food, clothes, and all the necessities for her family and household. Initiative and hard work are the only ways to live and accomplish the goals of these verses.

The virtuous woman goes the extra mile for quality goods for her household and obtains the best she can with her resources. She sets the example for

TODAY'S VIRTUOUS WOMAN

her family and servants by rising early to begin her day. She uses her talents for everyone's well-being and has planned what is needed. She does not shirk from her responsibilities for the household, from the smallest child to the oldest servant providing daily guidance to them. Her family values the virtuous woman because they recognize the magnificent woman they have.

Not many women today spin yarn to make clothes for their families and servants. Most of our chores are easier due to modern conveniences. However, like the virtuous woman, we must plan and provide for our families. We must shop for the best quality food that we could afford. We ensure that everyone is clothed appropriately. We watch over our family daily and provide guidance and instruction for the entire household. Today's virtuous woman is responsible for the management and oversight of the household and home, just like this biblical woman.

Her Community and Church

She extends her hand to the poor, yes; she reaches out her hands to the needy (v. 20).

Her husband is known in the gates, when he sits among the elders of the land (v. 23).

The Proverbial Woman

Give her of the fruit of her hands, and let her own works praise her in the gates (v. 31).

In Bible times, there were no social welfare programs. Prisoners in jail had no lunchroom, doctors, or bed linens. Widows with no family did not have an income to sustain themselves and often starved to death. Disabled persons and orphans were often beggars in the street. The virtuous woman was concerned about the poor and needy, just as she was concerned for her household. She was involved and active in charity and community projects. She looked to see what she needed to do and did it! Foresight and planning were necessary to accomplish everything that the virtuous woman did. She led others to complete projects to benefit those in need.

Virtuous women are involved in their churches. Remember, God values everyone the same and expects all of us to work in His kingdom. He gave all of us work to do in His church (Gal. 3:28). Women don't get a pass related to work at church.

Our children must be taught both at home and in Bible classes. If we don't teach our children about God, someone else will surely educate them about the world. Bible class material must be prepared and presented, which provides teaching opportunities for many. Some may develop class and teaching materials better than others, while others prefer to lead the class and Bible discussions with the children. Thoughtful preparation to teach our children helps them to understand their faith and not just endure the church services sitting beside their parents.

Our sick and elderly in the congregation all need a virtuous woman's support and love. Visits, cards, and meals are not the only services that a virtuous woman

can provide to the sick and elderly. She can drive to doctor appointments, weed the flower bed, and go to the grocery. The virtuous woman will not forget the caregiver for those who cannot take care of themselves. The person providing daily care to their loved one needs our support as much as the unwell person.

All we must do is look in our community and churches to find our projects. There are needy people in the richest communities. What may be the biggest problem is to determine the specific project to tackle and not become overwhelmed by the needy of the world. Each woman should do what she can with her talents and resources.

The virtuous woman can provide help to her community and church because she is involved, has extended herself, and reached out to others. She has inventoried her skills and abilities and sought ways to work in God's kingdom. The hardest part of helping others may be looking past self and seeing the work to be done. There are plenty of opportunities and work for all virtuous women.

Her Qualities

Who can find a virtuous wife? For her worth is far above rubies (v. 10).

She seeks wool and flax, and willingly works with her hands (v. 13).

The Proverbial Woman

She also rises while it is yet night, and provides food for her household and a portion for her maidservants (v. 15).

She girds herself with strength, and strengthens her arms. She perceives that her merchandise is good, and her lamp does not go out by night. She stretches out her hands to the distaff, and her hand holds the spindle (v. 17-19).

She makes tapestry for herself; her clothing is fine linen and purple (v. 22).

Strength and honor are her clothing; she shall rejoice in time to come. She opens her mouth with wisdom, and on her tongue is the law of kindness. She watches over the ways of her household, and does not eat the bread of idleness (vv. 25-27).

Charm is deceitful and beauty is passing, but a woman who fears the Lord, she shall be praised (v. 30).

The virtuous woman has many admirable qualities to emulate, and sermons often quote Proverbs 31 for today's women. She is capable, willing, inquisitive, dedicated, industrious, talented, cheerful, energetic, loving, respected, generous, caring, convicted, reliable, dependable, analytical, eager, vigorous, efficient, honorable, smart, tactful, diplomatic, organized, charming, beautiful, and God-fearing. This list probably isn't long enough to describe this amazing woman!

What if God did not give you all these admirable qualities? How can you be like the virtuous woman when you do not have all her gifts? What if you are good with animals, but afraid of strangers? What if you are great at math, but cannot bake a cake? What if you are willing, but have a chronic disease limiting your mobility? What if you live in a small town with few Christians? What if you are poor without money to spend on good works?

Our biblical role model has many superb gifts and talents given to her by God that all of us do not have. That is not the point of the verses. The real lesson is what she does with her gifts and talents. She puts her words into action and doesn't just talk about the work that she is going to do. She does what she can and is busy early and late. She has gotten up from her couch, put down her Smartphone, and gotten to work. God knows what you have the capability of doing and does not expect more than we can do; however, He does expect us to do!

Verse 30 tells us that fearing God is the quality to be most desired. Sometimes society does not value this quality in a godly woman but prefers the sexy model or the hard-hitting entrepreneur. Love and respect for God is the virtuous woman's crowning achievement. She lets her light shine for

TODAY'S VIRTUOUS WOMAN

all to see, and her love for God is evident. Today's virtuous woman knows honoring God is the most vital quality for her!

Her Business Pursuits

She seeks wool and flax, and willingly works with her hands. She is like the merchant ships; she brings her food from afar. She also rises while it is yet night, and provides food for her household and a portion for her maidservants. She considers a field and buys it; from her profits she plants a vineyard (vv. 13-16).

She perceives that her merchandise is good, and her lamp does not go out by night (v. 18).

She is not afraid of snow for her household, for all her household is clothed with scarlet (v. 21).

She makes linen garments and sells them, and supplies sashes for the merchants (v. 24).

She opens her mouth with wisdom, and on her tongue is the law of kindness (v. 26).

In these verses, the virtuous woman is both the buyer and the seller. Let's first look at the buyer aspects of the virtuous woman.

The virtuous woman shops for items to benefit her household and willingly uses those products for the good of each person. She looks for the best that she can afford with consideration for her family and servants, not just herself. She is not afraid of snow, because she has prepared for winter weather with appropriate clothing for all. She uses her time and resources in a manner to get the most out of them as she procures goods for herself and her household.

As a seller, the virtuous woman has business interests within and outside her home. She buys a field for a vineyard and builds a profitable vineyard business. She sews and sells linen garments and sashes to merchants. The main point about the virtuous woman's business interest is that she sells quality goods and is an industrious woman.

Verse 26 describes how the virtuous woman conducts herself as she buys and sells. She does not have a sharp tongue with ugly words for vendors or her customers. The virtuous woman is known for being smart and kind. Being kind does not mean she lets others take advantage of her. It indicates she has chosen her words carefully and thoughtfully considered each business opportunity for her benefit and fairness to all.

Today women are pulled in many directions. Contemporary culture often values product consumption and careers over family life. Women are prodded to have the most stylish clothes, makeup, and hairstyles plus a luxurious home and a high-paying job, instead of valuing a lifestyle with a commitment to husbands and families. This priority is not how the virtuous woman looked at her business ventures as a buyer and seller. She considered how her activities affected everyone in her household and not just how they pleased her.

She did not demand luxuries for herself and make others do without or ask for things the family could not afford. Her business pursuits were for the family's benefit and not only the prestige of a successful company. She made long term plans for her financial resources and used her profits or income in the best manner that she knew how, with kindness and wisdom. These are the business lessons that we can derive from the virtuous woman.

Her Relationship with God

She girds herself with strength, and strengthens her arms (v. 17).

Strength and honor are her clothing; she shall rejoice in time to come (v. 25).

She opens her mouth with wisdom, and on her tongue is the law of kindness (v. 26).

Charm is deceitful and beauty is passing, but a woman who fears the Lord, she shall be praised (v. 30).

Verse 30 indicates that the essential aspect of the virtuous woman is the fear of the Lord. Proverbs 1:7 tells us, "The fear of the Lord is the beginning of knowledge, but fools despise wisdom and instruction." The fear of the Lord is a loving reverence for God that includes submission to Him and the commands of His word with honor and respect. The virtuous woman's faith in God is her support and shield for her life and the light that she shines for others to see. She gathers her strength in the wisdom from God and emulates His will by treating others with kindness.

Charm and beauty are used for both good and evil, but a virtuous woman only seeks good. God is the priority in her life, and her goal is to please God first.

Today godly women are often ridiculed for seeking God first. Honor and respect for the commands of God are not desirable qualities for many of today's sophisticated women. Maybe this sophisticated woman has God on her bucket list but hasn't checked Him off yet. Our contemporary culture often emphasizes beauty and riches above the fear of the Lord, so many do not consider God in their daily schedules.

The virtuous woman knew God demanded to be first in her life. He may have given the virtuous woman charm, beauty, riches, and all the pleasant things this world had to offer. However, she knew that all these earthly gifts were passing, and her heart rested with God. Strength and honor are her clothing; she opens her mouth with wisdom, and on her tongue is the law of kindness. These qualities are how the virtuous woman used her earthly gifts to honor and respect God and is our example today.

Conclusion

Today's virtuous woman can live a godly life using the Proverbial virtuous woman as a pattern and example. She actively pursued the things that she could do for her husband, family, household, and community while she honored God. God expects us to do what we can and knows what abilities we have. The most important lesson she teaches us is love and respect for God. This Proverbial virtuous woman is an example of today's virtuous woman!

The Proverbial Woman

Lesson 1

Discussion Questions

1. Is the virtuous woman of Proverbs 31 a relevant example for women today?

   Does God expect each of us to have all the qualities of this virtuous woman?

2. What are the qualities of the Proverbial woman?

   Of these qualities, which do you see in yourself?

   Should you see more of her qualities in yourself?

   If yes, then can you make an improvement plan?

3. Should women compare their works to the works of other Christian women?

   When would this comparison be a helpful thing to do?

   When would this comparison be damaging?

TODAY'S VIRTUOUS WOMAN

4. Who would have been in the household of the Proverbial woman?

   Who is in the household of today's virtuous woman?

   Is this difference an issue for today's virtuous woman?

5. How should a virtuous woman today treat people and businesses that provide her products and services?

6. Is charity an important quality of the virtuous woman?

   How can we be charitable today? Who should receive our charity?

7. Did the virtuous woman work outside of the home'?

   What kind of business pursuits are open to today's virtuous woman?

8. What is the most vital aspect of the virtuous woman?

   How can we emulate that quality in our lives?

Husband and Wife

Husband and Wife

Chapter 2—Husband and Wife

Discussion about the relationship between a husband and wife is more than talking about submission. A godly couple must appreciate and plan for all aspects of a healthy marriage relationship. Submission by itself is not a marriage and not what God intended for His creation. This discussion about the husband and wife includes picking a spouse, being "unequally" yoked, sex, roles of a husband and wife, and then finally, submission.

Picking a Spouse

The first thing my husband and I told our sons about choosing a wife is that she must help you get to heaven and this is the best advice for any unmarried person. A spouse that helps his or her mate get to heaven is truly wonderful! Good looks, brains, financial means, and social status are a poor second because those qualities do not have eternal value. If heaven is a Christian's goal, then picking a spouse based on earthly measures will not help achieve the goal of heaven. Abraham knew a faithful spouse was important for Isaac and took action to prevent Isaac from marrying an idol-worshipping Canaanite woman (Gen. 24:3).

Lesson 2 TODAY'S VIRTUOUS WOMAN

The beauty of a woman is the first thing a man may notice, and a handsome man will attract a woman's attention. However, the actions and the inner qualities of a person are much more essential for a life-long spouse. If the potential spouse is self-centered, greedy, and lazy before marriage, do not expect a wedding ring to change those qualities. Marriage is not a way to improve anyone. Look for good inner characteristics before marriage, not after! Someone who does not treat his date well before marriage will not treat a spouse well after marriage. Actions demonstrate the inner qualities of a potential mate.

For example, when Abraham's servant was sent to find a wife for Isaac, the sign he asked from God was action from the woman, not how she looked or what she wore (Gen. 24:1-27). The servant chose the woman for Isaac's wife based on her response to his request for a drink of water. The favored young woman, Rebekah, not only gave him water but watered his camels and invited him to stay at her father's house. The actions of this young lady demonstrated a lot about the type of person she was. She was someone who thought of others more than herself—a superb inner quality. Rebekah became Isaac's wife, and together they led godly lives.

Having the right person for a spouse makes both the husband and the wife better people and strengthens them for their work in God's kingdom. Abraham knew this when he made his servant promise that the chosen wife would not be a Canaanite (Gen. 24:3). The mother of King Lemuel knew that what was on the inside of the Proverbial woman was more important than beauty for the wife for her son (Prov. 31:1). It is essential to pick a spouse with interest in godly things, the fortitude to help others achieve heaven, and the appreciation of his spouse. Two people that have chosen a spouse well will always have someone to help them tackle life's problems as they make their journey to heaven.

Being Unequally Yoked

Christians are often married to non-believers. Maybe they married before living a godly life was critical to the Christian, maybe someone taught them the gospel after they married, maybe the unbelieving spouse has fallen away from living a righteous life, or maybe the Christian thought they could change the unbeliever after marriage. Any of these situations make a stressful marriage relationship as the two partners pull against each other about any religious issue.

Paul warns Christians against being united with unbelievers:

Do not be unequally yoked together with unbelievers. For what fellowship has righteousness with lawlessness? And what communion has light with darkness? And what accord has Christ with Belial? Or what part has a believer with an unbeliever? (2 Cor. 6:14-15).

Paul's point is that Christians and unbelievers are not the same and mingling together can be harmful to the Christian. Imagine a donkey yoked with an ox? Will this pair pull well together? A Christian and an unbeliever's beliefs and attitudes will be as dissimilar. Note that this warning is not limited to a marriage, but business and social situations as well.

However, often, Christians and unbelievers are married. In writing to the Corinthians, Paul said,

But to the rest I, not the Lord, say: If any brother has a wife who does not believe, and she is willing to live with him, let him not divorce her. And a woman who has a husband who does not believe, if he is willing to live with her, let her not divorce him. For the unbelieving husband is sanctified by the wife, and the unbelieving wife is sanctified by the husband; otherwise your children would be unclean, but now they are holy. But if the unbeliever departs, let him depart; a brother or a sister is not under bondage in such cases. But God has called us to peace. For how do you know, O wife, whether you will save your husband? Or how do you know, O husband, whether you will save your wife? (1 Cor. 7:12-16).

When a Christian is married to an unbeliever, the Christian spouse is a living example of the gospel message to the unbeliever. In this situation, the Christian is carrying a heavy load for the whole family as she works to teach and show what Christ has done for her and what it means to be a faithful Christian.

Sex

God fashioned man and woman for each other, and He intended a husband and wife to enjoy sex. After God made Adam and Eve, He saw that His creation was "very good" (Gen. 1:31). This conclusion included sex between Adam and Eve! The book Song of Solomon is about the love between Solomon and his Shulamite wife and describes their enjoyment of each other's bodies. The beauty and desirableness of sex between married couples is evident in the Bible. After all, in Genesis 2:25, we are told Adam and Eve were naked and not ashamed. However, a couple must work together to enjoy and have a good sex life within their marriage.

A punishment/reward system is not the basis of a Christian's sex life. Each partner should enjoy his or her spouse and learn to give oneself to the other. Paul said:

Let each man have his own wife, and let each woman have her own husband. Let the husband render to his wife the affection due her, and likewise also the wife to her husband. The wife does not have authority over her own body, but the husband does. And likewise the husband does not have authority over his own body, but the wife does. Do not deprive one another except with consent for a time, that you may give yourselves to fasting and prayer; and come together again so that Satan does not tempt you because of your lack of self-control (1 Cor. 7:1-5).

Sex in the marriage bed is the sharing of each other. God made sex a part of our lives and bodies. Yes, sex is part of procreation, but God made it good and meant for both the husband and wife to enjoy it.

Neither spouse owns the other's body and must be considerate of him or her. Christian husbands and wives are as thoughtful and loving to their spouses as they are to themselves.

Husbands, love your wives, just as Christ also loved the church and gave Himself for her . . . So husbands ought to love their own wives as their own bodies; he who loves his wife loves himself. For no one ever hated his own flesh, but nourishes and cherishes it, just as the Lord does the church . . . .

Husband and Wife

Nevertheless let each one of you in particular so love his own wife as himself, and let the wife see that she respects her husband (Eph. 5:25-29, 33).

When spouses love their partner as their own body, then the sexual part of the relationship has the greatest chance of pleasure and success for both the husband and wife. Both married partners treating each other with love, honor, and respect is how Christ treats His church. This message in Ephesians 5 is to married couples.

It is equally evident that sex outside of marriage is condemned and has been since the beginning of time. "Thou shall not commit adultery" is the 7th commandment given to Moses by God on Mount Sinai (Exod. 20:14). In the Old Testament, adulterers were put to death (both the man and the woman). Again, "The man who commits adultery with another man's wife, he who commits adultery with his neighbor's wife, the adulterer and the adulteress, shall surely be put to death" (Lev. 20:10). Modern-day birth control methods, our culture, and the media seem to encourage and applaud adultery, but this is not God's way. God intended sex to be enjoyed only within marriage.

Roles of a Husband and Wife

God made man and then made woman. Does this make a man superior to a woman? Genesis 2:18, the Lord God said, "It is not good that man should be

Lesson 2 TODAY'S VIRTUOUS WOMAN

alone; I will make him a helper comparable to him." Yes, God made man first and then woman as a comparable helper. The Merriam-Webster dictionary defines the word "comparable" as an adjective saying two or more things are very similar and can be compared to each other. God made man and woman, so they are helpful to each other, not one better than another. In God's plan, He values all humanity. "There is neither Jew nor Greek, there is neither slave nor free, there is neither male nor female; for you are all one in Christ Jesus" (Gal. 3:28). Every person is equally important to God.

So, if God values man and woman the same, are the roles of a husband and wife the same? No, their roles are not the same within the marriage, but neither are they unequal. The husband leads the family as Christ leads the church. For the husband is head of the wife, as also Christ is head of the church; and He is the Savior of the body (Eph. 5:23). No organization or marriage can have two leaders. They would be like the pushmi-pullyu, the fictional character in Dr. Dolittle, with two heads. Which head decides the direction to walk? The husband is the marriage leader in God's plan!

In our prior discussion of the proverbial woman in Proverbs 31, there were many facets of that busy example of a godly woman. A very concise list of roles for women is given Paul's epistle to Titus:

Husband and Wife

> *As for you, speak the things which are proper for sound doctrine . . . . older women likewise, that they be reverent in behavior, not slanderers, not given to much wine, teachers of good things that they admonish the young women to love their husbands, to love their children, to be discreet, chaste, homemakers, good, obedient to their own husbands, that the word of God may not be blasphemed* (Titus 2: 1, 3-5).

Women have much to do. However, the roles of wife, mother, and homemaker are the most important to a godly woman.

The husband and wife are life mates in a marital bond: "Therefore a man shall leave his father and mother and be joined to his wife, and they shall become one flesh" (Gen. 2:24). The man and woman don't desert their extended families but become a separate family unit—two people in a single new household. They must work together within their roles to have a successful Christian marriage.

Submission

Submission is to be obedient to some requirement or authority and is also a term for military order and rank. In marriage, the wife is submissive to her husband: "Wives, submit to your own husbands, as to the Lord" (Eph. 5:22). Remember, both the wife and husband are heirs of God, so one is not valued by God more than the other one is. However, the submission of the wife to the authority of her husband is required by God.

A godly man has a big task assigned to him by God. Notice the husband has more requirements in Ephesians 5:22-33 than do women:

> *Wives, submit to your own husbands, as to the Lord. For the husband is head of the wife, as also Christ is head of the church; and He is the Savior of the body. Therefore, just as the church is subject to Christ, so let the wives be to their own husbands in everything. Husbands, love your wives, just as Christ also loved the church and gave Himself for her, that He might sanctify and cleanse her with the washing of water by the word, that He might present her to Himself a glorious church, not having spot or wrinkle or any such thing, but that she should be holy and without blemish. So husbands ought to love their own wives as their own bodies; he who loves his wife loves himself. For no one ever hated his own flesh, but nourishes and cherishes it, just as the Lord does the church. For we are members of His body, of His flesh and of His bones. "For this reason a man shall leave his father and mother and be joined to his wife, and the two shall become one flesh." This is a great mystery, but I speak concerning Christ and the*

church. Nevertheless let each one of you in particular so love his own wife as himself, and let the wife see that she respects her husband.

The husband and wife both have demanding roles. These roles are complicated when both parties are working hard to be godly. The difficulty increases ten-fold when one party does not fulfill his or her entire responsibility in God's marriage plan or is not a Christian. Does this end the marriage? No, it does not. The godly example of partner may influence the weaker one in the marriage to see God's way is better and help him or her to obtain heaven. Paul tells this to us in 1 Corinthians 7:16, which says, "For how do you know, O wife, whether you will save your husband? Or how do you know, O husband, whether you will save your wife?"

God knew man needed a woman and made the marriage bond. When a wife submits to her husband's family leadership, she is submitting to God and being obedient to God's authority and law. "Submit yourselves therefore to God" (Jas. 4:7a). In this manner, today's virtuous wife is like the Proverbial wife. The heart of her husband safely trusts her (Prov. 31:11).

Discussion Questions

1. What qualities make a good spouse? How do these qualities help the married couple get to heaven?

   Did the husband in Proverbs 31 help his wife get to heaven?

   Did he have qualities that make a good spouse?

2. How can someone know if the person she is dating will make a faithful spouse?

3. Can a person be a fervent Christian when married to an unbeliever? Can this couple have a strong marriage?

Husband and Wife

Lesson 2

What problems might this couple have? How could those problems be overcome?

4. Can a Christian spouse convert an unbelieving spouse?

   What happens if they cannot?

5. Can a marriage survive adultery?

6. Must a virtuous wife yield to all her husband's sexual requests?

   Must the husband?

7. What is a submissive wife in today's culture?

   Is that the same or different than the Proverbial wife?

8. What other topics can be included in a discussion of husband and wife?

Motherhood and the Household

Lesson 3—Motherhood and the Household

Today's women often struggle with issues related to motherhood and homemaking. The invention of effective birth control has given women options for child-bearing that were unheard of by the Proverbial woman. Modern conveniences, grocery stores, take-out food, and cleaning services have changed homemaking. Nice homes and cars or meeting minimum financial requirements often make two incomes necessary.

As a member of the "older women" group mentioned in Titus 2:3, I am supposed to be "a teacher of good things." I have a mantra when asked about being a good wife and mother, "God, husband, kids, family, then everything else." Mantras are easy to say and hard to do.

Motherhood and the Household

Lesson 3

Let's spend a little time discussing a few issues about motherhood and homemaking for today's virtuous woman: namely, priorities for a virtuous woman, teaching our children about God, disciplining our children, motherhood with no father in the home, homemaking in the 21st century, working outside the home, and finally, hospitality.

Priorities for Virtuous Women

God has always been insistent that He is first in our lives. The first commandment given to Moses was, "You shall have no other gods before Me" (Exod. 20:3). The first four commandments all deal with man's relationship with God, and the last six are about man's interrelationships with each other (Exod. 20:3-17). God always is first in our lives! His priority in our lives is emphasized frequently in the New Testament.

> *But seek first the kingdom of God and His righteousness, and all these things shall be added to you (Matt. 6:33).*

> *And you shall love the Lord your God with all your heart, with all your soul, with all your mind, and with all your strength. This is the first commandment (Mark 12:30).*

Our husband is our next priority, as a marriage made a husband and wife "one flesh" (Gen. 2:24; Matt. 19:5-6). Sometimes we forget the marital bond, because of other demands of our life. Many times, a wife becomes a lioness with only consideration for her children or an entrepreneur building a thriving business. The marriage bond created before God can be easy to forget. Our husbands can fend for themselves, right? Sorry, but God does not see it this way.

> *Wives, submit to your own husbands, as to the Lord. For the husband is head of the wife, as also Christ is head of the church; and He is the Savior of the body. Therefore, just as the church is subject to Christ, so let the wives be to their own husbands in everything (Eph. 5:22-24).*

The wife's role is not smaller or less than the husband's; it is just different. She is the heart of the household, and the husband is the head. Both are necessary for a healthy marriage and a godly home.

Teaching Our children about God

Have you seen the billboard wishing that children came with an instruction manual? Well, there is one! The Bible is the virtuous woman's instruction manual for raising children. Teaching biblical things to our children is a must.

Did Moses, Timothy, and John the Baptizer learn to love God by themselves? No! Jochebed taught Moses in Pharaoh's palace. Eunice and Lois taught Timothy during difficult Jewish persecution of Christians. Elizabeth taught John the Baptizer while living under Roman rule and Herod's oppression. These women could teach their children to love God because they loved and knew God themselves.

> *And these words which I command you today shall be in your heart. You shall teach them diligently to your children, and shall talk of them when you sit in your house, when you walk by the way, when you lie down, and when you rise up. You shall bind them as a sign on your hand, and they shall be as frontlets between your eyes. You shall write them on the doorposts of your house and on your gates* (Deut. 6:6-9).

While we are teaching our children to love God and using the Bible for our basis, we are teaching them how to live and how to treat others. The best way to teach our children is by example!

> *He who says he abides in Him* ought *himself also to walk just as He walked* (1 John 2:6).

Motherhood and the Household

The goal is to teach our children to walk in their own life as Jesus walked in His—obeying God, doing good things, and loving others. We can demonstrate what we are teaching by being an example of godly living.

Disciplining our children

Discipline for our children is hard for all parents. It is difficult to know the best thing to do as we are raising our children. The parents can have different opinions for situations due to their personal history. These differences require insight and discussion from both parents to have a united approach to raising their children. Sometimes it is just easier to let the television, psychologists, or schools decide how our children should act. Being our children's friend is always easier than being their parent.

Proverbs has many verses to encourage parents about their children's discipline.

But the person who loves his children is careful to correct them (Prov. 13:24b).

Discipline and teach your son while there is hope (Prov. 19:18a).

The rod and reproof give wisdom, but a child left undisciplined brings his mother to shame (Prov. 29:15).

Paul compares God's discipline to a father's discipline in Hebrews 12:7-11.

If you endure chastening, God deals with you as with sons; for what son is there whom a father does not chasten? But if you are without chastening, of which all have become partakers, then you are illegitimate and not sons. Furthermore, we have had human fathers who corrected us, and we paid them respect. Shall we not much more readily be in subjection to the Father of spirits and live? For they indeed for a few days chastened us as seemed best to them, but He for our profit, that we may be partakers of His holiness. Now no chastening seems to be joyful for the present, but painful; nevertheless, afterward it yields the peaceable fruit of righteousness to those who have been trained by it.

Paul is writing that parents who love their children train and discipline them! Discipline is both positive and negative. Also, discipline is not the same for all children, but appropriate for each child. A verbal reprimand may be sufficient, but spanking may also be required. The Bible warns parents about undue harshness in children's discipline.

And you, fathers, do not provoke your children to wrath, but bring them up in the training and admonition of the Lord (Eph. 6:4).

> *Fathers, do not provoke your children, lest they become discouraged* (Col. 3:21).

While these last two verses are written directly to the fathers, they apply to both fathers and mothers. Parents must train their children in the ways of the Lord, instructing them how to live in our world. Appropriate discipline is part of this training.

Motherhood with no Father in the Home

Today many households have no father in the home. The marriage has ended in divorce, the parents never married, the mother is a widow, or the husbands travel for work or are deployed in the military. For whatever reason, there is not a consistent father in the home, and the mother is responsible for all aspects of providing for and managing the household.

When most or all the demands of raising godly children rest on the mother's shoulders, the best advice is to continue to serve the Lord. Teaching children about God, supervising homework and chores, participating in school activities, and being responsible for providing for the family are huge responsibilities. The struggle to get everyone to worship and put God as a priority in daily lifestyles is real. However, the long-range reward for teaching our children about God is so important to all the family.

There is an old proverb "As is the mother, so is her daughter." This proverb would also apply to mothers and sons. Similarly, children who see a mother who works hard to provide for them while serving the Lord are more likely to live by her example when they are adults. Remember, your children's spiritual development will save their souls. Daily demands and paying bills can hamper your vision of this goal but getting to heaven is the true goal for everyone.

There are biblical examples of mothers who taught their children to love God with little or no help from the fathers of their children. Eunice taught Timothy to love God and had a Greek husband (2 Tim. 1:5). John Mark's mother, Mary, had the house where people were praying for Peter's release from prison

Motherhood and the Household

(Acts 12:12-17). The Bible does not mention her husband. John Mark went with both Paul and Barnabas on missionary journeys to teach others the gospel. These mothers had taught their sons to love the Lord! Teaching our children to love God is the goal for today's mothers, too.

Another idea is having your children around faithful men who can be examples of Christian living for your children. A mother can teach her children a lot, but she won't have a true "manly" perspective. Don't let the media be all your children know about manly roles and responsibilities.

Blended Families

Today many families are blended with shared children. Geography, time, lifestyles, and faith may all be different in each household where a child spends part of his life. Everyone that loves that child is affected by all decisions related to that sharing. These situations are too varied and complicated to discuss fully in this lesson. However, today's virtuous woman must approach these situations as would Jesus, who said, "A new command I give you: Love one another. As I have loved you, so you must love one another" (John 13:34).

We must love that child and all the "shared" family in the self-sacrificing way that Christ loved us. Respect for all involved parties is a keystone in all communication and actions.

Homemaking in the 21st century

Wikipedia defines homemaking as the management of a home, the act of overseeing the organizational, day-to-day operations of a house or estate, and the managing of other domestic concerns. However, Wikipedia is missing what the Bible wants women to do related to homemaking.

Homemaking in the 21st century is so different than it was for the Proverbial woman when we only consider the chores related to homemaking. Today we have malls and grocery stores and bakeries. We have refrigerators, automatic stoves, vacuum cleaners, and microwave ovens. We even have Amazon, which makes it easier to "obtain food from afar" (Prov. 31:14)!

God wants us, women, to set the tone for our households. Yes, we have chores to do, food to prepare, and clothes to wash. However, women are the nurturers looking after the members of our homes. We teach children. We offer hospitality. We give love and compassion while we organize the chaos of modern family life. As stated in a prior section, the wife and mother is the heart of the family, and the husband is the head. She influences all parts and members of a household. This influence is what God considers to be the most important part of homemaking.

Emphasizing this influence is the purpose of these two verses in Titus 2. "Admonish the young women to love their husbands, to love their children, to be discreet, chaste, homemakers, good, obedient to their own husbands, that the word of God may not be blasphemed" (vv. 4-5). The home and homemaking are such important parts of God's plan for man here on earth.

Working outside the home

Today the gulf between "stay-at-home" moms and "working" moms is huge. Both sides often accuse the other of grievous shortcomings. First, let me tell you that I was a working mom. That was the choice for my husband and I and not the choice for everyone else. I realize that I benefitted from the work of full-time homemakers who volunteered at my children's school, made Bible study material, and were working hard in God's kingdom. Don't get into a finger-pointing fight. There is no single answer for all us ladies. Remember, God is the ultimate One that we must please with our choices, and our goal is to get to heaven to be with Him.

In the example of the Proverbial woman, she worked in the home and outside the home. She both "watched over the ways of her household" (31:27) and "bought a field and from her profits, she planted a vineyard" (31:16). Women have biblical responsibility for the household, but they are supposed to work on earth and in the kingdom. In Titus 2:5, women are told to be homemakers, so the word of God is not blasphemed. In 1 Timothy 5, young widows are counseled to marry, to have children, to manage their homes, and to give the enemy no opportunity for slander.

Paul wrote, "If anyone will not work, neither shall he eat" (2 Thess. 3:10). The context of this verse teaches that idleness is a cause of sin. All are to work in

Motherhood and the Household

the kingdom. So, can a woman instructed by God to be a homemaker work for wages or profit outside of the home?

Each woman has diverse opportunities, skills, and abilities as God made each of us differently. He knows what we can do and what we cannot do. In the parable of the talents (Matt. 25:14-30), the master gave each servant some money. To one he gave five talents, to another he gave two talents, and to the last, he gave one talent. The first point for us in this parable is that the master expected each servant to use the master's money well. The second point is that the master was aware of the servants' abilities. The master expected each servant to work to make a return on the master's investment. He knew that he gave the servants different amounts of money, and they had different abilities. Still, he expected them to work for him with what they had!

One woman may choose to be a full-time homemaker, while another may choose to work outside the home. Neither choice is right or wrong. The real issue is, are we working in the kingdom? With whatever choices we make, we must serve God, respect our husbands, and maintain a godly home. None of us are the same, have the same opportunities, or have the same abilities or interests. We do have the same God whom we must serve. Taking a full-time job outside the home may be your choice or a requirement. However, God and your home are your greater priorities.

Hospitality

Who has time to invite people to your house? Who has money to pay for dinner out with guests? Not me! Maybe someone else, but I am too busy to prepare and plan for anything like that. After all, others have more money and time plus a nicer place than I do.

Do these comments sound familiar? Surely not! Those first Christians after Pentecost, who lingered in Jerusalem to learn about the new covenant with God would have suffered if the resident Christians had felt like these comments. Acts 2:46-47 tells us, " So continuing daily with one accord in the temple, and breaking bread from house to house, they ate their food with gladness and simplicity of heart, praising God and having favor with all the people. And the Lord added to the church daily those who were being saved." The local Jerusalem Christians opened their homes and their pocketbooks to provide for all those thousands of new "out-of-town" Christians. A disciple living in Jerusalem named Joses provided so much for these Christians that they gave him a new name, Barnabas, meaning "son of encouragement" *(Acts 4:36).* He continues to be a worthy example of hospitality for us today!

During the beginning of Christianity, saints in the Jerusalem church were stretched in attempting to support Hellenistic, i.e., non-local disciples. The first chapters of Acts contains many examples of Christians helping Christians during this exciting time. Our opportunities for hospitality may not have drama and historical impact, but we do have opportunities. It is equally important that we have an attitude about hospitality that is like the 1st century Christians.

Be hospitable to one another without grumbling (1 Pet. 4:9).

This verse commands us to be hospitable to show love for others. "And above all things have fervent love for one another" *(1 Pet. 4:8).* With hospitality, we demonstrate that we are using the gifts that God has given us to serve Him.

Probably the best verse about hospitality comes from Hebrews 13:2, which says, "Do not forget to entertain strangers, for by so doing some have unwittingly entertained angels." Take pleasure in being hospitable and enjoy your guests!

One last idea about hospitality. Do the following comments sound familiar? "Oh, don't bother with dinner for me, because I don't want to inconvenience anyone. I will get a hotel room and won't disturb your family."

Let people be nice to you. Be gracious when someone shows hospitality to you. Maybe you accept the hospitality, or maybe you don't. However, consider your reasons for your decision and decide whether that decision reflects Christ's love for others.

Motherhood and the Household

Lesson 3

Discussion Questions

1. If your husband is not a Christian or not a faithful Christian, how can God be your priority?

2. Is your husband always more important than your children or your job?

   Is there a difference, in the husband's priority in your life and his role during certain instances?

3. What are some good methods for teaching our children about God?

   Have the parents failed God if their children do not follow God? Why or why not?

4. How do we reconcile "Do not provoke your children to wrath" and "Spare the rod, spoil the child"?

5. What would a mother who is leading her household alone need from other Christians?

   How can we offer that support?

6. How is being the "heart of the household" involved in homemaking?

   Why does the author propose that homemaking is more than a tidy house and home-cooked meals?

7. Can "working outside the home" get in the way of homemaking?

   What can "working" wives and mothers do in these situations?

8. How can you show hospitality other than hosting a group in your home?

9. Are we required to sell our property as Barnabas did to help other Christians? If not, what else should we do?

Money Management

Lesson 4—Money Management

When did money management become a ladies' class topic? Since God made Eve as a *helpmeet* for Adam! God expected Adam and Eve to take care of His creation then, and He expects us to take care of His creation now. Everything we have belongs to God, including our assets, and we must manage them wisely. The Proverbial woman was a careful money manager as she bought and sold merchandise, food, and fields and managed her household. Today we must manage our money carefully, too.

In ancient times, many believed that riches were a sign of God's blessings and the goodness of a person. Conversely, poverty and disease were considered a sign of sinfulness. Jesus taught that this idea is not true! In Matthew 5:45, Jesus says, "He makes His sun rise on the evil and on the good, and sends rain on the just and on the unjust."

God knows what resources are available to us and the ability we have to use those resources. He expects us to work daily in His kingdom using those resources and abilities. Jesus teaches about this in the parable of the talents

(Remember a talent was money in Bible times).

For the kingdom of heaven is like a man traveling to a far country, who called his own servants and delivered his goods to them. And to one he gave five talents, to another two, and to another one, to each according to his own ability; and immediately he went on a journey (Matt. 25:14-15).

Each servant received different amounts of money and had different abilities to use the money. In verse 30, the servant who had hidden the money given to him by the master was called an "unprofitable servant" because he made no effort to use the money for the master's gain. The master meant for *all* his servants to use the money and resources given to them to be profitable in His kingdom. How can today's proverbial woman be a profitable servant to God and manage His money well?

Wise Use of Money

The Proverbial woman provides excellent examples of wise money and asset utilization. She was like merchant ships bringing the food to her household (v. 14). She watched over her household for efficiency and wastefulness (v. 27). She used her money to buy a field and make a profit with it (v. 16) and produced quality merchandise (vv. 18, 24). This woman worked tirelessly to manage her money and her household.

No matter what money we have, God expects us to remember the correct priority that money has in our life—God before money!

Then He spoke a parable to them, saying: "The ground of a certain rich man yielded plentifully. And he thought within himself, saying, 'What shall I do, since I have no room to store my crops?' So he said, 'I will do this: I will pull down my barns and build greater, and there I will store all my crops and my goods. And I will say to my soul, Soul, you have many goods laid

Money Management

up for many years; take your ease; eat, drink, and be merry.' But God said to him, 'Fool! This night your soul will be required of you; then whose will those things be which you have provided?' So is he who lays up treasure for himself, and is not rich toward God" (Luke 12:16-21).

God did not condemn the rich man for having lots of crops and goods. God condemned the man for forgetting God owned his soul and everything that he possessed and for depending on himself and his riches instead of God. Instead of many years to enjoy his prosperity, the man had one day. A person can have many earthly possessions and still be poor toward God. This rich man did not understand that all he owned belonged to God, who expected the rich man to have his priorities in order and use His money wisely.

Remembering that God is more important than money was too hard for a young man who met Jesus on the road in Judea (Luke 18:18-27). This young man who was rich and a ruler in his community asked Jesus what he needed to do to get to heaven. The young man had proudly kept the Old Law and assumed Jesus would be impressed with his accomplishments. Jesus knew this young man's heart and how much he enjoyed his privileged life and status in the community. The rich young ruler was dejected when Jesus told him to sell all that he had and follow Him. Jesus required top priority in the young man's

life, and the young man couldn't do that. His riches and status were more important to him than God.

God requires two things from all of us—to be first in our lives and to work in His kingdom. To do both things requires prioritizing the wise use of all money, resources, and assets that we have on earth to God's glory. As we manage these things, we must always have God first in our hearts.

Knowing Your Financial Requirements and Status of Your Finances

The Proverbial woman could not have managed her money and household; if she didn't plan what she was going to do and how she was going to do it. Proverbs has many wise sayings related to money management. A few of these verses follow.

> *Prepare your outside work, make it fit for yourself in the field; and afterward build your house* (Prov. 24:27).

> *Be diligent to know the state of your flocks, And attend to your herds; For riches are not forever, Nor does a crown endure to all generations. When the hay is removed, and the tender grass shows itself, And the herbs of the mountains are gathered in, The lambs will provide your clothing, And the goats the price of a field; You shall have enough goats' milk for your food, For the food of your household, And the nourishment of your maidservants* (Prov. 27:23-27).

> *The wise woman builds her house, But the foolish pulls it down with her hands* (Prov. 14:1).

The most basic step of money management is *knowing* your financial requirements and available resources. The admonition, "Prepare your outside work" (Prov. 24:27), demands knowledge of the requirements for the work to be done in the field, methods to accomplish the work, the materials required to do the work, and the cost of it. No one can run a household or business without knowing what the costs are for the household or business. "Knowing the state of your flocks and gathering from the fields" (Prov. 27:23-27) is constant attention to your resources. Gathering the food from the fields, wool from the sheep, and milk from the goats all entail continual awareness about those fields and flocks. How can you know about a sickness affecting your flocks, if you are not paying attention to the sheep and goats? How can you know about pests in your crops, if you are not paying attention to the fields? You can't! You can't know your financial health either if you are not paying attention.

Money Management

Lesson 4

How does the last proverb in the above list relate to wise money management? Overspending weakens the finest household, and uncontrolled debt will "pull down" the house. Don't spend more than you have! Any home can have lean times, even hard times. Just ask our relatives about living during the Great Depression to learn about hard times! During the Great Depression, most households struggled to meet even their most minimum requirements. Today's proverbial woman must understand her financial requirements, her budget, and her resources to avoid pulling her house down by overspending.

We can overspend even during good times. Impulsive or emotional buying wrecks a budget. That sweet pair of boots may make your new outfit, but can you make the rent payment? Your granddaughter wants to go to that concert, but what about your grocery bill? The Proverbial woman probably spoiled her children and herself occasionally with extras, but first, she knew and met the requirements of her household. She planned to meet her household requirements and knew about delayed gratification for those extras.

God expects us to pay our bills. All of them! Romans 13:7 commands, "Render therefore to all their due: taxes to whom taxes are due, customs to whom customs, fear to whom fear, honor to whom honor." Make your payments when they are due. Today with credit cards and online banking, money is invisible and magical. Don't fall into this trap of ignoring these "invisible" bills. Know your financial requirements and know your assets.

A person can develop debts and bills that are significantly larger than their assets. Today, these persons can go before a bankruptcy judge. Bankruptcy is being legally judged to be unable to pay off personal debts. Is bankruptcy sinful? This author thinks that it is. The debtor agreed to pay each accumulated debt—bankruptcy results in unpaid debts. Jesus said, "Let your 'Yes' be 'Yes,' and your 'No,' 'No'" (Matt. 5:37). Your word should be enough that lenders know you will pay all the money owed to them.

When your assets do not cover your requirements, trust God. In Matthew 6:25-26, Jesus teaches, "Therefore I say to you, do not worry about your life, what you will eat or what you will drink; nor about your body, what you will put on. Is not life more than food and the body more than clothing? Look at the birds of the air, for they neither sow nor reap nor gather into barns; yet your heavenly Father feeds them. Are you not of more value than they?"

When you are in financial straits, you must first assess your situation to plan how to pay your debts and what changes to make. Communicate with your lenders to develop a payment plan. Do the best you can and know that it may take a long time to resolve your financial situation. Remember, God didn't put out the fire for Shadrach, Meshach, and Abed-Nego. He put Jesus in there with them (Dan. 3:19-25).

Get Good Advice

Sometimes we women need financial advice. Getting good advice is essential. How does the Bible help us with that? Jethro's advice to Moses helped Moses resolve problems among the Israelites by selecting and organizing godly men to judge the people (Exod. 18). Joseph's advice to Pharaoh resulted in storehouses of grain to feed Egypt during the seven years of famine (Gen. 41). King

Money Management

Rehoboam heeded bad advice resulting in a revolt and a divided kingdom in Israel (1 Kings 12).

How can we know that we have chosen a good advisor? One way is to use the same criteria that Jethro advised Moses to use to pick leaders to judge the Israelites: "Moreover, you shall select from all the people able men, such as fear God, men of truth, hating covetousness; and place such over them to be rulers of thousands, rulers of hundreds, rulers of fifties, and rulers of tens" (Exod. 18:21).

Using similar qualifications for our financial advisors would be as advantageous to us as it was for Moses and his judges.

Able men

Your best friend may love you forever, but do they know anything about money management? Your best friends may even have your best interest in their hearts. However, to plan for a more complex circumstance, you may need a more trained advisor.

Such men as fear God

Someone who fears God is going to have a similar perspective to the use of God's money as a virtuous woman does. What this person would understand is all money belongs to God, and we are just temporary "owners" of it. This type of advisor would understand a godly woman's priorities about the use of her money.

Men of truth

An advice-giver that does not value truth is not necessarily going to be truthful to you. This person must be looking out for your interest and not someone else's interest when advising you. Someone with questionable loyalties may not give you the best advice.

Hating unjust gain

Some of the versions render this, "Choose men . . . who hate a bribe." Bribes or cheating are not desirable qualities for our advisor. Anyone who walks the razor edge of legality is not an advisor for any proverbial woman!

Greed and Covetousness

Our financial goals cannot be only to increase our wealth. Throughout time, God has warned His people about the hunger for earthly things and materialism. Christians must use their worldly possessions for God's purposes. Probably one of the most popular verses quoted to warn about greed is in Paul's first epistle to Timothy:

> *Now godliness with contentment is great gain. For we brought nothing into this world, and it is certain we can carry nothing out. And having food and clothing, with these we shall be content. But those who desire to be rich fall into temptation and a snare, and into many foolish and harmful lusts which drown men in destruction and perdition. For the love of money is a root of all kinds of evil, for which some have strayed from the faith in their greediness, and pierced themselves through with many sorrows* (1 Tim. 6:6-10).

Greed and covetousness are not only problems for certain classes of people but are "equal opportunity sins" for all. God wants us to be content with what we have and not let our desires here on earth blind us to our real goal of heaven. When we let our desires to become more important than God, we can go down paths leading to sin.

These verses are not teaching that working hard for your family, home, education, or other goals in your life is sinful. Rather, they emphasize that God must be leading your life, not hard work, or goal achievement. These verses clearly warn us of this danger.

> *Do not lay up for yourselves treasures on earth, where moth and rust destroy and where thieves break in and steal; but lay up for yourselves treasures in heaven, where neither moth nor rust destroys and where thieves do not break in and steal. For where your treasure is, there your heart will be also* (Matt. 6:19-21).

God knows that we must have food, shelter, and clothing. He also knows there are many beautiful things on this earth, and some people have a lot of those beautiful things, and others do not have so much. Whichever is our situation, God wants to be first in our lives and for us to be content.

Charity and Giving Back to God

Discussion of our management of God's money would not be complete without a discussion of charity toward others and giving back to God. Proverbs 11:25 teaches that giving to others is good for the giver: "The generous soul will be made rich, and he who waters will also be watered himself." Charity gives to both the receiver and the giver.

Money Management

The next paragraph is from James Coffman in his commentary related to Ruth.

> The Law of Moses had laid down strict rules protecting the right of the poor to glean following the reapers. These are spelled out in Leviticus 19:9; 23:22; and in Deuteronomy 24:19. Landowners were forbidden to reap their fields out to the very borders, nor could they send the reapers a second time into the same field. If they overlooked a bundle of grain, they were forbidden to go back and get it. Similar rules also applied to the harvest of vineyards and orchards. The purpose of this was to allow the poor an opportunity to provide for themselves. This was the legal background of Ruth's gleaning (Coffman, notes on Ruth 2:2).

After Pentecost, many Christians lingered in Jerusalem to learn more about Christ and His kingdom. The early Christians took up collections to help other Christians in need. The book of Acts has many examples of charity among these early Christians. We also see charity directed toward Paul and the apostles along with directions about caring for widows and orphans. Christians are supposed to help others.

God wants us to be charitable because we have tender hearts and see a need. He does not want us to be charitable to get honor and prestige from other people.

> *Take heed that you do not do your charitable deeds before men, to be seen by them. Otherwise, you have no reward from your Father in heaven. Therefore, when you do a charitable deed, do not sound a trumpet before you as the hypocrites do in the synagogues and in the streets, that they may have glory from men. Assuredly, I say to you, they have their reward. But when you do a charitable deed, do not let your left hand know what your right hand is doing, that your charitable deed may be in secret; and your Father who sees in secret will Himself reward you openly* (Matt. 6:1-4).

Lastly, God wants us to give back to Him. Everything we possess already belongs to God, and God knows that we have needs on earth. However, God wants us to share in the work of the kingdom and giving money toward the work in His kingdom is part of our share.

> *Now Jesus sat opposite the treasury and saw how the people put money into the treasury. And many who were rich put in much. Then one poor widow came and threw in two mites, which make a quadrans. So He called His disciples to Himself and said to them, "Assuredly, I say to you that this poor widow has put in more than all those who have given to the treasury; for they all put in out of their abundance, but she out of her poverty put in all that she had, her whole livelihood"* (Mark 12:41-44).

God knows what the widow and the rich gave to the temple treasury. The amount given is not what God deems most significant, but the value of the gift to the giver. Good stewardship of our earthly assets demands that we also fulfill our spiritual obligations and contribute to the work in God's kingdom.

Money Management

Lesson 4

Discussion Questions

1. Are the rich more blessed by God than the poor? Why or why not?

2. Why does the author include money management as part of our work in God's kingdom?

3. What did Jesus know about the value of money within the rich young ruler's life (Luke 18:18-27)? How does this apply to us today?

4. Why do you think the woman in Proverbs 31 was a good or bad money manager?

5. What is the correct way for a husband and wife to manage their money?

6. How can the wife cause unnecessary strain in a family budget? The husband?

7. Must we use a paid financial advisor to get good advice?

8. Do all paid advisors give good advice?

9. Who can give good financial advice?

10. How can greed and covetousness become part of a financial plan or budget?

11. How far must we go to help another Christian?

12. Considering the widow with two mites in Mark 12, what else should we consider when we are giving toward the work in God's kingdom?

13. What advice would you give to another based on your "lessons learned'?

Charity and the Community

Chapter 5—Charity and the Community

Charity is an emotionally charged subject for most people. Some people believe in minimal charity as "all should work for what they get." Others want everyone to have anything they want because everyone should have their dreams. Another person wants to help some people that are "worthy" but not "unworthy" people. These are just a few ideas people have about charity, and I know each reader could add to this list. However, does the Bible have anything to tell us about charity?

The answer to that question is a resounding "YES"! The Scriptures have guidance and examples of charity throughout their pages. One of the best-known verses is Galatians 6:10, which says, "Therefore, as we have opportunity, let us do good to all, especially to those who are of the household of faith."

So, let us first consider how to "do good" to the household of faith and then how to "do good" to all.

Household of Faith

God expects all Christians to help other people. After all, this is one of the distinctions between a Christian and the world. Christians demonstrate God's

TODAY'S VIRTUOUS WOMAN

love with their love and care for people. Of course, in the above verse, Christians are to provide charity to other Christians. Christians are our family, our adopted brothers, and sisters in Christ, and God expects us to treat them like family.

Our closest family in the household of faith is those in the group with whom we worship. How can we be of assistance if we have no idea what their problems are? News alert—the ONLY way to know what those opportunities are is to spend time with our brethren. This knowledge does not come by ESP. If you limit your conversations to only a few in the congregation, then your opportunities to "do good" are just as limited.

However, there is a second side to obtaining knowledge of opportunities to "do good" among our close family of faith. The person with the problem must share it with the brethren. Sometimes sharing this knowledge can be so hard! Our problems can be so personal that sharing is embarrassing. We feel that we caused our situation and aren't deserving of help from Christians. There are so many reasons to keep the details of our problems to ourselves. However, no one can help you when they do not know about the need. One solution is to confide in an elder or a trusted member of the congregation and get advice on how to proceed. God did not mean for us to face our problems alone. He gave us a Christian family to help us, even if there is not a full solution to the shared problem.

Charity and the Community

Of course, there are Christians throughout the world, and we cannot have a personal relationship with all of them. God wants us to help as we become aware of the need and have the means to do so. For example, the Christians in Galatia provided for the Christians in Jerusalem who were experiencing a famine (1 Cor. 16:1-3). In this instance, the Galatians collected money to send to Jerusalem to buy food.

Examples happening among Christians today are helping after a natural disaster, praying for Christians abroad, providing financial support for a preacher in another country or state. I am aware of individuals providing money directly to other Christians to buy food during a drought and to dig a well. There are many ways for individuals to provide charity and support to other Christians. Each of us is in a different situation with different opportunities to help another. Remember that God knows all this, but He wants all Christians to extend themselves when they can.

In Philippians 4:10, Paul praises the Philippians for sending charity to him when they could: "I rejoiced in the Lord greatly that now at last your care for me has flourished again; though you surely did care, but you lacked opportunity." Notice he politely lets them know he is aware that they always have cared about his work, but can only now send money. These Philippians help Paul when they have the opportunity. Prayer is also supporting another Christian!

Good to All

"Good to all" is also in Galatians 6:10. "All" includes a lot of people! Is a Christian responsible for helping every person in the world? First, we don't know all the people in the world. Second, we physically, emotionally, and financially cannot help all of them. That would be a crippling endeavor. Realistically we cannot respond to all the needs just in our city or county. How then can we obey God's command to do "good to all"?

We "do good" as we have the opportunity and the means. Christians are the salt of the earth (Matt. 5:13), and we are supposed to change the world! The salt can't season the stew unless sprinkled into the pot. Neither can a Christian influence if we don't show the world what a Christian is.

God loves the entire world and wants the world to know the good news of the gospel. In John 3:16, Jesus said, "For God so loved the world that He gave His only begotten Son, that whoever believes in Him should not perish but have everlasting life." God wants the whole world to know His love and how to obtain salvation from sin. When Christians "do good to all," they are teaching the world about the gospel.

While we are occupied doing good, we are teaching the world how to be a Christian. We do what we can and as we have the opportunity. Noticing urgent opportunities within our communities and helping practically and efficiently is a way to show others how a Christian is different than the world.

> *And let our people also learn to maintain good works, to meet urgent needs, that they may not be unfruitful (Titus 3:14).*

By showing love and charity, a Christian shows God's love to others. It is a righteous work for Christians to help other Christians and other people with their urgent needs. God knows each of us. He knows what we have at our disposal and what we can do and will judge us accordingly. Remember, in the parable of the talents, the master knew the capabilities of each servant and had realistic expectations for each (Matt. 25:14-30). That master was God, and we are the servants. God expects all His servants to work in His kingdom.

Jesus and Charity

Charity toward others is important. When we are serving others, we are serving God. Charity and service are almost interchangeable words when "doing good" in God's kingdom. Jesus highlights this in the 25th chapter of Matthew:

> *Then the King will say to those on His right hand, "Come, you blessed of My Father, inherit the kingdom prepared for you from the foundation of the world: for I was hungry and you gave Me food; I was thirsty and you gave Me drink; I was a stranger and you took Me in; I was naked and you clothed Me; I was sick and you visited Me; I was in prison and you came to Me." Then the righteous will answer Him, saying, "Lord, when did we see You hungry and feed You, or thirsty and give You drink? When did we see You a stranger and take You in, or naked and clothe You? Or when did we see You sick, or in prison, and come to You?" And the King will answer and*

say to them, "Assuredly, I say to you, inasmuch as you did it to one of the least of these My brethren, you did it to Me" *(vv. 35-40).*

When Christians help Christians and other people of the world, we are serving our Lord! Jesus frequently taught about having a servant spirit and being a servant to others.

Charity Requires Planning and Action

The woman in Proverbs 31 shows us that charity involves planning and action from the individual assisting. Verse 20 says, "She extends her hand to the poor, yes, she reaches out her hands to the needy." Notice in this one verse, there are TWO active verb phrases—extends her hand to the poor and reaches out to the needy. She had considered the needs of her household and the needs of those in the community. She had made an effort to know about the needs of others and then evaluated those needs. This woman did not help the poor and needy without effort and attention on her part.

Could she help everyone that she decided had a need? No, she couldn't. No one can do that. She would have determined who had an urgent need *(Titus 3:14)* and helped according to her capability *(Matt. 25:14-30).* In 2 Thessalonians 3:10b, Paul writes, "If anyone will not work, neither shall he eat." As the Proverbial woman was assessing the needs of others for urgency and her capability for helping them, she would have considered whether the person was making efforts to help themselves. If we have more than we need, God wants us to help other Christians. In 2 Corinthians 8:13-15, Paul wrote:

> *For I do not mean that others should be eased and you burdened; but by an equality, that now at this time your abundance may supply their lack, that their abundance also may supply your lack—that there may be equality. As it is written, "He who gathered much had nothing left over, and he who gathered little had no lack."*

Paul and the Proverbial woman lived in different biblical eras but assessing the needs of others and our capabilities to help them is no different for us today. God wants us to have a charitable attitude toward others and to make charity and service a part of our lifestyle. We must reach out to the needy and extend our hand to the poor. We always have loving hearts and set aside part of our time and resources to help others.

Attitude toward Charity

Our personal feeling toward service and giving to others is as important as the activity itself. God wants us to give our resources and time to help others

as freely and lovingly as He gives His gifts to us. Our charity must be without compulsion and regret. In 2 Corinthians 9:6-8, Paul teaches God loves a cheerful giver and takes care of those who give.

But this I say: He who sows sparingly will also reap sparingly, and he who sows bountifully will also reap bountifully. So let each one give as he purposes in his heart, not grudgingly or of necessity; for God loves a cheerful giver. And God is able to make all grace abound toward you, that you, always having all sufficiency in all things, may have an abundance for every good work.

People can perform or give charity for many reasons. One reason is to honor God, and another reason is to obtain honor from men.

Honor from others must not be our goal as it was for Ananias and Sapphira when they gave money to feed others (Acts 5:1-11). After Pentecost, many of the early Christians had lingered in Jerusalem to learn more about the gospel. Some Jerusalem Christians sold their land to provide money to feed and house these brethren. Ananias and Sapphira wanted some of that glory and sold land, too. They donated money to the cause but lied about the price of their land to make their sacrifice seem greater to other Christians. Their unrighteous desire for praise from men resulted in lying to God and their deaths.

A man who lived during this same time was named Joses (Acts 4:36-37). He sold his land and donated the proceeds to the apostles also. The difference in Joses's donation and Ananias and Sapphira's is that Joses gave God the honor and glory with the donation. His goal was to serve and honor God and not to obtain glory for himself. Joses was renamed Barnabas by the apostles (i.e., "Son of Encouragement"), because of his fervent service to God.

Getting a newspaper article about your service and charity is not necessarily sinful. Your service to others may be newsworthy. However, there is a dif-

Charity and the Community

ference in service to men and service to God. Primarily that difference starts in your heart and leads to your attitude. When honor from men is your real goal, then you are not honoring God. The goal is to show the world how a Christian lives and to glorify God in our charitable acts.

The good Samaritan is a great example of charity with a generous heart. The Samaritan found a beaten stranger on the road. He gave immediate aid to the beaten man, transported him on his donkey to an inn, arranged and paid for care for the beaten man, and later checked on the recovery of the man. The Samaritan helped this man knowing that the beaten man could not repay him, nor would the Samaritan get an award for his actions. This Samaritan had a generous heart and helped the man because he could.

Generosity

God has always wanted man to share his wealth with less fortunate people. The Law of Moses had many laws to protect and provide for the poor. For example, in Old Testament times, part of any harvest was left for the poor to glean for themselves. Boaz instructed his workers to drop extra grain for Ruth to glean because he was so impressed with her devotion to Naomi.

Solomon writes a lot about a generous heart, and his Proverbs guide giving to others. Some examples are

There is one who scatters, yet increases more; and there is one who withhold more than is right, but it leads to poverty. The generous soul will be made rich, and he who waters will also be watered himself (Prov. 11:24-25).

He who despises his neighbor sins; but he who has mercy on the poor, happy is he (Prov. 14:21).

He who has pity on the poor lends to the Lord, *and He will pay back what he has given (Prov. 19:17).*

He who has a generous eye will be blessed for he gives of his bread to the poor (Prov. 22:9).

Solomon teaches us that we are enriching ourselves when we give to others. Paul expressed the same idea: "But this I say: He who sows sparingly will also reap sparingly, and he who sows bountifully will also reap bountifully" (2 Cor. 9:6). God does not want His Christians to be stingy givers! He knows a generous spirit is good for the giver.

Can showing mercy and providing help to the poor make a person happy? Absolutely! Compassion for others is a trait that God emphasizes so many times. It is strange how giving to someone else makes the giver glow within his or her own heart. Generosity is a trait that God loves. Remember in 2 Corinthians 9:7, God loves a cheerful giver.

Who would not be willing to lend money to God? Solomon is teaching that charity is the same as lending money to God. Everyone knows God will pay His debt with all the appropriate interest. Remember all that we have belongs to God anyway. God wants each Christian to purpose in his heart to be charitable with God's own money. Being generous with money that belongs to God anyway is how God wants us to approach charity.

Our Attitude When Receiving Charity

What should be our attitude about receiving charity? One of our best examples may be Paul when he received support from the Philippians.

> *But I rejoiced in the Lord greatly that now at last your care for me has flourished again; though you surely did care, but you lacked opportunity. Not that I speak in regard to need, for I have learned in whatever state I am, to be content: I know how to be abased, and I know how to abound. Everywhere and in all things I have learned both to be full and to be hungry,*

Charity and the Community

both to abound and to suffer need. I can do all things through Christ who strengthens me. Nevertheless you have done well that you shared in my distress . . . Not that I seek the gift, but I seek the fruit that abounds to your account. Indeed I have all and abound. I am full, having received from Epaphroditus the things sent from you, a sweet-smelling aroma, an acceptable sacrifice, well pleasing to God (Phil. 4:10-18).

We must be grateful for help from others when they can provide it and be satisfied when desired help isn't on the horizon. Our pride may make it hard to see charity as a "sweet-smelling aroma." That pride can work in more than one way. It can be a part of us which works hard to overcome our circumstance. Or it can be sinful by not giving God the glory for the care provided to you. It pleases God when His people are charitable, and it pleases Him when the recipient is grateful for the gift. God wants us to be grateful for the support provided by others and to know that God is the source of that blessing.

Whenever possible, thank the person providing the service to you. After healing the ten lepers in Luke 17:11-19, Jesus marveled that only one leper who was a Samaritan returned to thank Him for the healing. Even Jesus liked a "thank you"!

God does not want His people to depend on charity to live. He means for all to work for their bread. "If anyone will not work, neither shall he eat" (2 Thess. 3:10). However, God also knows that earthly circumstances leave some people in want. He has told His people to look out for and provide help to those less fortunate. None of us live in isolation, and God wants His family to look out for each other. We communicate with each other, help each other, and pray for one another. We help those who have a need whenever we can. That is God's plan.

Church or Individual Responsibility?

Some feel that charity is a work of the church and not the individual. The work of the church is evangelism (Matt. 28:19-20), the edification of Christians (Heb. 10:24-25), and benevolence for saints (Gal. 6:9-10). So yes, charity is a work of the church. However, the work of the church does have limits.

In 1 Timothy 5, Paul writes, "Honor widows who are really widows . . . . Now she who is really a widow, and left alone, trusts in God and continues in supplications and prayers night and day . . . But if anyone does not provide for his own, and especially for those of his household, he has denied the faith and is worse than an unbeliever" (vv. 3-5). This is an example that the church is limited and that the individual Christian is not. The church would not provide support to a widow that has children, but the individual Christian is unlimited in charity, which they decide to provide to the widow.

God wants His people to have loving, giving hearts, to extend our hand to the poor, and to reach out our hands to the needy just as the woman in Proverbs 31.

Discussion Questions

1. How can we know the needs of the Christians with whom we worship?

2. Must Christians tell their local congregation of all their needs?

3. How can we know about the needs of non-local Christians?

4. How can we "do good to all"?

   Must we use all our available resources to please God?

5. Why would Jesus say that charity toward others is serving Him (Matt. 25:34-40)?

6. Why is planning required for charity?

Charity and the Community

7. Why did the author talk about "action" related to charity?

8. What are the reasons that people perform charity? What does the Bible teach should be our reasons?

9. Why is charity good for the one performing the charity?

10. Why is the attitude of the recipient of charity important? Why would God care about that?

11. What are examples of charitable opportunities for an individual that a church would not perform?

Prayer

Chapter 6—Prayer

Hannah may be the most moving example of a woman and her prayers in the Bible (1 Sam. 1:1-28). She prayed to God to bear a son with all her heart, longing, and emotion. Hannah was so involved in her prayer that Eli, the high priest, thought she was drunk. She was moving her lips, but Eli heard no words! Hannah was not drunk, and God heard *every* word of her prayer. Hannah earnestly prayed for a son because she believed God could and did answer prayer. An angel from God told Hannah that God would answer her prayers for a son. Hannah praised God, who she knew answered prayers!

Today Christians are often uncertain about the effectiveness of their prayers. There are no angels delivering messages for God, divinely appointed apostles are not declaring the miracle is from God, and Jesus's apostles have not laid hands on anyone today for miraculous abilities. However, we can see the Bible tells us to pray for the things that we want and need. Does God listen to or do anything with those prayers?

Does God Answer Prayer Today?

Hannah was praying for God's help in her life. She had been married for many years and was barren during an era when a woman's worth was measured by the sons she had born. God answered Hannah's prayer with the birth of Samuel. Hannah received God's help, but can we pray for such help today?

Prayer

Lesson 6

The time of miracles has passed with the apostles' deaths. The purpose of these miracles was to confirm the message of the person performing the miracle. The first-century miracles proved that the gospel preached by the apostles was true and from God.

> *So then, after the Lord had spoken to them, He was received up into heaven, and sat down at the right hand of God. And they went out and preached everywhere, the Lord working with them and confirming the word through the accompanying signs (Mark 16:19-20).*

However, in our current times, we have the full gospel revealing the mystery of Christ's plan for salvation (Eph. 1:9). The miracles in the Bible confirmed the truth of the gospel. In 1 Corinthians 13:10, Paul writes, "But when that which is perfect has come, then that which is in part will be done away." When the whole gospel was made known to us, then that which is perfect had come, and the time for miracles to confirm the word, such as the ones performed by the apostles, was past.

Does God answer prayer today? Yes, God answers prayer! Do not underestimate the providence and power of God! We must have faith that God answers prayer and to pray for righteous things. Do not become inundated with concern about how God answers our prayers. God answers righteous prayer.

> *Now, this is the confidence that we have in Him, that if we ask anything according to His will, He hears us. And if we know that He hears us, whatever we ask, we know that we have the petitions that we have asked of Him (1 John 5:14-15).*

Righteous Prayer

Esther is a great example of our attitude toward God as we pray. She knew that if she approached King Ahasuerus without receiving his favor that she would die (Esth. 4:11). She approached Ahasuerus with profound reverence, awe, and honor due to a human king. Should we not approach God with similar emotions? God desires our presence and wants His people to desire His presence. Righteous prayer is our way of approaching God to receive His favor.

Jesus told the apostles in Mark 11: 24, "Therefore I say to you, whatever things you ask when you pray, believe that you receive them, and you will have them."

Does the above verse give us a blank check to ask for whatever we want? Will God give us anything we ask as long as we believe that He will give it to us? It teaches neither of those ideas. Jesus said, "Therefore do not be like them. For your Father knows the things you have need of before you ask Him. In this manner, therefore, pray . . . " (Matt. 6:8-9). Our Lord wanted His followers to know how to pray. Our Bibles have lessons about prayer to guide us in making appropriate requests to God.

John 14:14 teaches that we must ask in Jesus's name: "If you ask anything in My name, I will do it."

John 15:7 teaches that the person offering the prayer must belong to Him: "If you abide in Me, and My words abide in you, you will ask what you desire, and it shall be done for you."

1 John 3:22 teaches obedience is a requirement for answered prayer: "And whatever we ask we receive from Him, because we keep His commandments and do those things that are pleasing in His sight."

James 4:3 teaches that we cannot ask for selfish desires: "You ask and do not receive, because you ask amiss, that you may spend it on your pleasures."

Mark 9:23b teaches that we must believe our prayer is possible: "If you can believe, all things are possible to him who believes."

Matthew 7:7 teaches us to request what is important to us continually: "Ask, and it will be given to you; seek, and you will find; knock, and it will be opened to you."

Matthew 6:5 teaches us to pray humbly: "And when you pray, you shall not be like the hypocrites. For they love to pray standing in the synagogues and on the corners of the streets, that they may be seen by men. Assuredly, I say to you, they have their reward."

Matthew 6:7 teaches us not to pray mindlessly: "And when you pray, do not use vain repetitions as the heathen do. For they think that they will be heard for their many words."

Prayer

Lesson 6

James 5:16 teaches that the praying person must belong to God and be passionate about the prayer: "The effective, fervent prayer of a righteous man avails much."

James 5:13-15 teaches us to pray for specific needs: "Is anyone among you suffering? Let him pray. Is anyone cheerful? Let him sing psalms. Is anyone among you sick? Let him call for the elders of the church, and let them pray over him, anointing him with oil in the name of the Lord. And the prayer of faith will save the sick, and the Lord will raise him up. And if he has committed sins, he will be forgiven."

James 5:16 teaches us to pray for others: "Confess your trespasses to one another, and pray for one another, that you may be healed."

Mark 6:5-6 demonstrates that our unbelief limits God's power to us: "Now He could do no mighty work there, except that He laid His hands on a few sick people and healed them. And He marveled because of their unbelief. Then He went about the villages in a circuit, teaching."

Above all, God wants us to pray to Him and ask! "If you then, being evil, know how to give good gifts to your children, how much more will your Father who is in heaven give good things to those who ask Him!" (Matt. 7:11). Again, Paul said, "Be anxious for nothing, but in everything by prayer and supplication, with thanksgiving, let your requests be made known to God; and the peace of God, which surpasses all understanding, will guard your hearts and minds through Christ Jesus" (Phil. 4:6-7).

Parts of a Prayer

Prayers can have several sections in them with many points or ideas in each section. Prayers do not require each section, nor do the sections have to be in a particular order. Suggested sections are:

- **A**doration—Praises to God
- **C**onfession—Our confessions to God
- **T**hanksgiving—Thankfulness to God
- **S**upplication—Our requests to God

A person may ask why God needs to have praises and thankfulness in our prayers. After all, God knows all that He does and has done. The point of that part of the prayer is that God wants you to remember what He has done! The person praying needs to remember who God is before making requests to Him. Let's look at some prayers in our Bibles to see these sections.

In Matthew 6:9b-13, Jesus teaching His apostles to pray:

- ADORATION: "Our Father in heaven, Hallowed be Your name. Your kingdom come. Your will be done on earth as it is in heaven" (vv. 9-10).

- SUPPLICATION: "Give us this day our daily bread. And forgive us our debts, as we forgive our debtors. And do not lead us into temptation, but deliver us from the evil one" (vv. 11-13a).

- ADORATION: "For Yours is the kingdom and the power and the glory forever. Amen" (v. 13b).

Consider also Nehemiah's prayer before approaching Artaxerxes (Neh. 1:5-11).

- ADORATION: And I said: "I pray, Lord God of heaven, O great and awesome God, You who keep Your covenant and mercy with those who love You and observe Your commandments" (v. 5).

- CONFESSION: "Please let Your ear be attentive and Your eyes open, that You may hear the prayer of Your servant which I pray before You now, day and night, for the children of Israel Your servants, and confess the sins of the children of Israel which we have sinned against You. Both my father's house and I have sinned. We have acted very corruptly against You, and have not kept the commandments, the statutes, nor the ordinances which You commanded Your servant Moses. 8 Remember, I pray, the word that You commanded Your servant Moses, saying, 'If you are unfaithful, I will scatter you among the nations'" (vv. 6-7).

- THANKSGIVING: "But if you return to Me, and keep My commandments and do them, though some of you were cast out to the farthest part of the heavens, yet I will gather them from there, and bring them to the place which I have chosen as a dwelling for My name. Now these are Your servants and Your people, whom You have redeemed by Your great power, and by Your strong hand" (vv. 9-10).

- SUPPLICATION: "O Lord, I pray, please let Your ear be attentive to the prayer of Your servant, and to the prayer of Your servants who desire to fear Your name; and let Your servant prosper this day, I pray, and grant him mercy in the sight of this man" (v. 11).

Contemplate Hezekiah's prayer after Rabshakeh's threats (2 Kings 19:15-19).

- ADORATION: Then Hezekiah prayed before the Lord, and said: "O Lord God of Israel, the One who dwells between the cherubim, You are God, You alone, of all the kingdoms of the earth. You have made heaven and earth" (v. 15).

- SUPPLICATION: "Incline Your ear, O Lord, and hear; open Your eyes, O Lord, and see; and hear the words of Sennacherib, which he has sent to reproach the living God. Truly, Lord, the kings of Assyria have laid waste the nations and their lands, and have cast their gods into the fire; for they were not gods, but the work of men's hands—wood and stone. Therefore they destroyed them. Now therefore, O Lord our God, I pray, save us from his hand, that all the kingdoms of the earth may know that You are the Lord God, You alone" (vv. 16-19).

Types of Prayers

There is no reason to get complicated about the types of prayers. There are short and long prayers. There are public and private prayers. Prayers contain anything that the praying person wants to bring to God's attention or to ask of God. The items included in prayer are as numerous as the stars in the sky! So short, long, public, and private are the types of prayers for our discussion.

The most poignant short prayer must be the one by Jesus as He hung on the cross. "Father, forgive them, for they do not know what they do" (Luke 23:34). Our prayers can be arrows to God with our most heartfelt requests.

They do not need to be elaborately worded prayers to be heard by God. Short prayers can punctuate your day as you pray for yourself and others.

There are several examples of long prayers in the Bible, such as Nehemiah 9:5-38, 1 Kings 8:22-53, and John 17:1-26. Nehemiah 9:5-38 is the longest prayer in the Bible. It includes statements about God's great mercy in the history of the people of Israel and the confession of sins and disobedience. In 1 Kings 8, Solomon is dedicating the new temple with praise and thankfulness to God. In John 17, Jesus is praying for Himself, His disciples, and all believers. Your prayers can be long when God's help and guidance are needed or when praise and thankfulness fill your heart.

Public prayers are in front of a group of people, such as a worship service, class, or club. In 1 Kings 8:22-53, Solomon speaks a prayer in the presence of all the congregation of Israel to dedicate the temple. This prayer has praises and requests to God with much thoughtful wording. Jesus often prayed in public. His prayer before He raised Lazarus from the dead was to give praise to God and request belief from those watching the miracle.

Jesus said, "Father, I thank you that You have heard Me. And I know that You always hear Me, but because of the people who are standing by I said this, that they may believe that You sent Me" (John 11:41b-42). We women may not lead prayer in worship assemblies (1 Cor. 14:34-35). However, that does not prevent us from public prayers at other times!

God desires private prayers! In the Sermon on the Mount, Jesus tells the listeners, "When you pray, go into your room, and when you have shut your door, pray to your Father who is in the secret place; and your Father who sees in secret will reward you openly" (Matt. 6:6). Our prayers can be private, even if others know that we have separated ourselves to pray. When Jesus prayed in the garden of Gethsemane, He left His disciples some distance away so that He could pray privately (Matt. 26:36). Daniel prayed three times a day in an upper room in his

Prayer

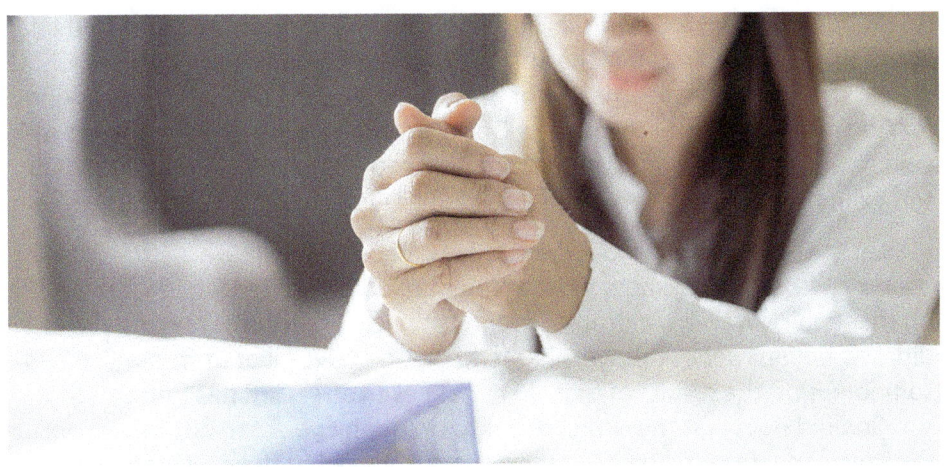

home, which Babylonian officials knew (Dan. 6:10). Our private time with God is the best way to grow closer to Him: "Draw near to God and He will draw near to you" (Jas. 4:8). Jesus and Daniel's examples show us this.

David has the most prayers in the book of Psalms (which warrant a separate detailed study). It is important to note that these prayers address many concerns that affect us today; safety, guidance, faith in God's promises, help in times of trouble, thanksgiving, forgiveness, repentance, mercy, and so many urgent needs. There are prayers of thankfulness, prayers of sadness, and prayers of happiness and joy. God does not limit our topics in prayers!

Attitude is the most important part of praying. God wants us to have a prayerful attitude and always pray: "Rejoice always, pray without ceasing, in everything give thanks; for this is the will of God in Christ Jesus for you" (1 Thess. 5:16-18).

Getting That for Which You Pray

Often, we pray for healing for our family, or we pray for a healthy birth, or we pray for world peace. Then our family member dies, or the child is born with a handicap, or another war erupts. Did God not hear our prayer? Was our prayer not righteous?

In Matthew 26:36-44, Jesus asked God not to require Him to die the cruel death of crucifixion. He prayed three times, "Let this cup pass from me." But each prayer also included, "Let Thy will be done." No one wants to be tortured and killed, and Jesus in His earthly body did not want pain either. However, Jesus prayed a righteous prayer. He made His request but also prayed, "Let Thy will be done." Jesus accepted crucifixion as God's will.

In 2 Samuel 12:16, David prayed for the healing of his son. Nathan had told David that God would cause the baby's death due to David's sin with Bathsheba. The king prayed earnestly for his son's healing for seven days by asking for God's grace. After the baby died, David washed himself and went to worship God (v. 20). Was David or his prayer not righteous? Yes, both were righteous. In this example, it was God's will that David's son would die because of David's sin.

Let's make up an example. We can pray for safety while we are driving cross country. We will never know what accidents God prevented while we were on that trip. However, if a drunk driver hits the car and causes major injury, did God not answer our prayer? Remember, God gave all of us free will. When someone sins, the results of that sin remain even after God has forgiven that sin. God did not want the drunk driver to sin nor hit your car, but He will not take away the drunk's free will. How can we know what the providence of God did for us during that trip while we are on this earth?

Recently an acquaintance asked me to pray for her daughter, who was in jail for possession of methamphetamines. I agreed to pray for her daughter, but for what should I pray? I cannot ask for her not to find the drugs or to get out of jail as that is her free will or the laws of the land. God wants her to abstain from drugs, but He will not stop her from choosing this lifestyle. I agreed to pray for her daughter's strength to abstain from drugs and for her to seek God's help. God will help with our battles but will not remove those battles.

My mother is an excellent example of righteous prayer. At the age of 72, she was diagnosed with Lou Gehrig's Disease and died five months later. I am certain that she prayed for healing. I know I prayed! I am also certain that her influence showing God's grace to others and finding joy in her tribulation was immense. God's providence allowed her to influence innumerable people by her faith in God. She and I did pray for her healing, but we also prayed that God's will to be done.

Let's offer a last example for which I do not have the final answer about whether God answered the prayer. A person is snow skiing down a hill and hits an icy patch, which causes him or her to slide uncontrollably toward trees. This person is earnestly praying to God to stop their collision with the trees. God made gravity, snow, hills, and ice—which make skiing possible. He made the metaphysical rules, which caused the momentum of the skier and the icy patch. The person has the free will to ski.

If the person hits the trees and is hurt, is that God's will? If the skier avoids the trees, is that God's will? God made the world and all that is in it. He set

Prayer

things in motion, which makes our world work, such as gravity. The person may hit the trees because the skier's abilities cannot overcome the momentum of the skier. Maybe the skier can divert himself to miss the trees. While on earth, we cannot know which events are caused by the providence of God and which are results of the chaos on our earth. We do know that God answers the fervent prayers of righteous people.

> *Behold, the Lord's hand is not shortened, That it cannot save; Nor His ear heavy, That it cannot hear (Isa. 59:1).*

> *Rejoice always, pray without ceasing, in everything give thanks; for this is the will of God in Christ Jesus for you (1 Thess. 5:16-18).*

Romans 8:26 has one of the best assurances about prayer in the Bible. God answers our prayers because our God is an awesome God who keeps His promises.

> *For we do not know what we should pray for as we ought, but the Spirit Himself makes intercession for us with groanings which cannot be uttered. Not knowing what to say or how to say it is not a problem when we make earnest petitions to God. The Spirit Himself takes our prayers upon Himself and intercedes for us with God.*

Discussion Questions

1. How can a righteous person pray for unrighteous things?

2. What was the purpose of Biblical miracles?

3. Does God perform miracles today? Why or why not?

4. What are the differences in a miracle and the providence of God?

5. What considerations must we make before praying to God?

6. How do doubt and indifference affect our prayers?

7. If God knows what we need, why should we pray?

8. Why are the parts of a prayer important? **A**doration—Praises to God, **C**onfession—Our confessions to God, **T**hanksgiving—Thankfulness to God, **S**upplication—Our requests to God

9. How do you know what type of prayer is necessary? Should we pray for things when we cannot know if God will do as we ask?

Personal Outlook and Our Reputations

Chapter 7—Personal Outlook and Our Reputations

The verses about the virtuous woman of Proverbs 31 teach us that who a woman is on the inside shows on the outside. Who she was within herself bloomed into her persona within her family and community and became her reputation. Let's consider our outlook and our reputations from the following perspectives.

- **Within ourselves**
- **Within the family and among the people who know us**
- **Public image**
- **Our legacies**

Within Ourselves

What and how we think about ourselves is very important. God loves us and wants us to know we are worthy of His love. However, we are not to be "in love" with ourselves. The beatitudes in the Sermon on the Mount help us learn to be the type of person God wants us to be on the inside (Matt. 5:3-12).

Blessed Are the Poor in Spirit (v. 3).

"Poor in spirit" is a person who is not conceited or arrogant and knows they need God. A good illustration of this quality is Jesus's parable of the Pharisee and the tax collector (Luke 18:9-14). The Pharisee's prayer included more praises for himself than for God. The tax collector knew he needed God, and his prayer reflected that knowledge. Jesus told us to be like the humble tax collector and not the haughty Pharisee.

Blessed Are Those Who Mourn (v. 4).

Life's trials often cause grief and mourning for all of us while we live on this earth. We grieve when our loved ones die or when we face huge losses in our life. We may mourn for our sin, the sin of others, or the evils of this world. God wants His people to look to Him for comfort during our grief and tribulation. This verse promises, "They shall be comforted." When Christians mourn while on this earth and lean on God during those trials, He is always there to comfort them. David and his psalms are wonderful examples of leaning on God for comfort during our trials.

Blessed Are the Meek (v. 5).

The use of the word "meek" in this verse is hard to understand today. The Bible often describes Jesus as meek. Meek does not mean physically or spiritually weak. The adjectives in Matthew 11:29 may be easier for us to understand the concept of the word meek: *gentle and humble in heart*. Meekness does not signify weakness but identifies one who is *gentle and humble in heart*. God wants His people to be spiritually strong with gentle and humble hearts as Jesus was.

Blessed Are Those Who Hunger and Thirst for Righteousness (v. 6).

God wants us to be people that desire righteousness. He wants us to crave what He offers and to strive to be obedient to His guidance. Those who hunger and thirst for righteousness long to be like Jesus. This inner quality is the intense desire to be as Jesus was—obedient to God's will.

Blessed Are the Merciful (v. 7).

Mercy is our attitude and the resulting actions toward other people. Mercy is forgiveness, but mercy is also how we treat people. After someone has treated us cruelly, it can be hard to be merciful in our reaction to them. In Matthew 6:15, Jesus teaches that we must forgive others for God to forgive us. Of course, we must be merciful to those with whom we live, but sometimes we must be merciful to those who have died. For example, remember someone who abused you that is not with you anymore. Do the stories you tell about that person reflect forgiveness from you to that person? Study Matthew 6:15 and 5:7 again to see how mercy and forgiveness from us to others are necessary to obtain mercy from God.

Blessed Are the Pure in Heart (v. 8).

"Pure in heart" means those who are faithful to God. Our heart is the center of our consciousness. When our faith fills that center, then we are pure in heart. No one can see inside us to examine how faith fills our consciousness, but our purity is observable to others. This inner quality ensures that *we will see God*.

Personal Outlook and Our Reputations

Lesson 7

Blessed Are the Peacemakers (v. 9).

This verse promises that someone with the inner quality of a peacemaker shall see God. To be the type of person who helps others to get along peaceably is a champion indeed! There are so many ways to exercise this quality—between members of our families, work teams, communities, and nations. Peacemaking is also bringing peace or eliminating strife in an individual's heart. In this sense, peace is reconciliation with God and is the best peacemaking of all!

Blessed Are Those Who Are Persecuted for Righteousness Sake (v. 10).

Persecution for righteousness's sake is not an inner quality, but a result of those qualities. Righteous people are often targeted by evil because of their righteousness. In 1 Peter 4:16, Peter encourages us to remain righteous as we endure persecution because our righteousness glorifies God: "If anyone suffers as a Christian, he is not to be ashamed, but is to glorify God in this name." The apostles found joy in their persecution and praised God during their hard times.

Each of the Christian inner qualities outlined in the beatitudes has a promise from God. The kingdom of heaven, mercy, and comfort from God, inheritance as God's child, righteousness, and peace are all ours because God has promised them to us. Our faith in these promises feeds us as we pursue the qualities that God desires in us.

Within the Family and among the People That Know Us

The sweetest melody for any woman is the section of Proverbs 31 describing the proverbial woman's reputation to her husband, her family, and her community.

> *The heart of her husband safely trusts her; so he will have no lack of gain. She does him good and not evil all the days of her life* (vv. 11-12).

> *Strength and honor are her clothing; she shall rejoice in time to come. She opens her mouth with wisdom, and on her tongue is the law of kindness. Her children rise up and call her blessed; Her husband also, and he praises her* (vv. 25-28).

This description of this woman is the goal for us all. Trust, goodness, strength, honor, wisdom, kindness, and love all contribute to this woman's reputation in her family and throughout her community.

Trust

In verse 11, the husband's heart trusts his proverbial wife to prudently and effectively manage his household so that he does not resort to ill-advised means to provide for the household. Other translations say, "for he shall have no need of spoil." Spoil would be oppressing tenants or slaves to obtain wealth, cheating, anything to maintain the lifestyle of the wife. This husband trusts his wife with his entire worldly means. This trust (or lack of thereof) would become the basis for the reputation of both the husband and wife. It also fuels the household dynamic. The trust of a good man for a good woman makes both the man and woman better.

Goodness

The proverbial woman "does good" for her husband and her family. Goodness is wanting the best for all family members. All women want good things for their family as the warm glow of a successful family reflects well on any woman. However, this goodness is a self-sacrificial love—the wife/mother freely gives of herself to care for those she loves. These are the women whose children call them "blessed" and whose husband "praises" them.

The next phrase of verse 12 tells us the proverbial woman does not do evil for her husband. This phrase is not talking about the evil in horror movies, but the way that the wife treats her husband and family every day. There are so many ways any woman can do evil to her husband or family. She can be wasteful of the family assets. She can demand more from her husband than he can provide. She can manipulate her children instead of nurturing them.

Personal Outlook and Our Reputations

Lesson 7

She can announce every shortcoming of the household. This attitude naturally becomes part of the woman's and her household's reputation within the community.

Women with goodness in their reputation are very aware of the "golden rule" as Jesus taught during the Sermon on the Mount: "Therefore, whatever you want men to do to you, do also to them, for this is the Law and the Prophets" (Matt. 7:12). The golden rule teaches us to pursue what is best for others. We must do so actively and energetically. It is much more than abstaining from treating people badly.

Strength and Honor

Verse 25 tells us that strength and honor are the clothing of the proverbial woman. Strength is not only muscular power and vitality. This strength comes from within the woman based on the knowledge of God's might and guidance for her. She has courage in her knowledge of right and wrong, which honors both her and God. She lives within her strength and honor until it is as comfortable to her as jeans and a T-shirt. A reputation based on these qualities is a goal for us today.

Joyful

The last half of verse 25 is easy to overlook. Sometimes it can be hard to find joy in our lives, but the proverbial woman "rejoiced in time to come." Women who find joy in hard times are beacons to their family and community. Remember how the apostles found joy in beatings and imprisonment? People who find joy during hardship are examples of confidence in God's grace.

Wisdom and Kindness

These two qualities are discussed together in verse 26 and particularly mention the mouth and lips of the proverbial woman. Using care and thought before she spoke, ensured wisdom and kindness are in the words of proverbial woman.

TODAY'S VIRTUOUS WOMAN

How we speak to and about others is of great concern to God and directly affects our households and reputations. The book of Proverbs has a lot to teach us about speaking to others. Some of these Proverbs follow.

Not Whining and Complaining

A continual dripping on a very rainy day and a contentious woman are alike (Prov. 27:15).

Thoughtful

A soft answer turns away wrath, but a harsh word stirs up anger (Prov. 15:1).

The wise in heart will be called prudent, and sweetness of the lips increases learning (Prov. 16:21).

Encouraging

Pleasant words are like a honeycomb, sweetness to the soul and health to the bones (Prov. 16:24).

Anxiety in the heart of man causes depression, but a good word makes it glad (Prov. 12:25).

Honest

Better is the poor who walks in his integrity than one who is perverse in his lips and is a fool (Prov. 19:1).

Humble

Whoever falsely boasts of giving is like clouds and wind without rain (Prov. 25:14).

Love

The word "love" is not in the verses about the proverbial woman. However, *agape* love is evident within this

Personal Outlook and Our Reputations

household. *Agape* love is the unconditional, self-sacrificing care and concern for another without expecting anything in return. *Agape* love is a choice that motivates action. Women with this love in their hearts will have a great reputation anywhere they live and work, as glory is not their motivator.

Love for others is the standard that Jesus taught His disciples and is a commandment for us. "A new commandment I give to you, that you love one another; as I have loved you, that you also love one another. By this, all will know that you are My disciples, if you have love for one another" (John 13:34-35). This same commandment is our standard as virtuous women today. When we choose to obey Jesus and have *agape* love, we must consider others' needs.

Public Reputation

Our public reputation starts with our outlook and how we see our self. It develops and is sustained by how we treat our family members, our coworkers, our Christian brothers and sisters, and anyone we meet. God cares about our reputations! If we warm the church bench on Sunday and cheat our customers on Monday, God cares. If we sing hymns on Sunday and belittle our husband on Tuesday, God cares.

> *Even a child is known by his deeds, by whether what he does is pure and right* (Prov. 20:11).

> *A good name is to be chosen rather than great riches, loving favor rather than silver and gold* (Prov. 22:1).

God wants His people to have loftier goals than the fleeting riches and glory of this earth. His people should be distinctive while on earth due to their actions, and His guidance in those actions should be evident. God wants His people to have godly reputations. In Romans 12, Paul writes some clear instructions to us about behaving as Christians.

> Let love be without hypocrisy. Abhor what is evil. Cling to what is good. Be kindly affectionate to one another with brotherly love, in honor giving preference to one another; not lagging in diligence, fervent in spirit, serving the Lord; rejoicing in hope, patient in tribulation, continuing steadfastly in prayer; distributing to the needs of the saints, given to hospitality Bless those who persecute you; bless and do not curse. Rejoice with those who rejoice, and weep with those who weep. Be of the same mind toward one another. Do not set your mind on high things, but associate with the humble. Do not be wise in your own opinion. Repay no one evil for evil. Have regard for good things in the sight of all men. If it is possible, as much as depends on you, live peaceably with all men. Beloved, do not avenge yourselves, but rather give place to wrath; for it is written, "Vengeance is Mine, I will repay, " says the Lord. Therefore "If your enemy is hungry, feed him; If he is thirsty, give him a drink; For in so doing you will heap coals of fire on his head." Do not be overcome by evil, but overcome evil with good (vv. 9-21).

These instructions summarize how Christians treat each other and everyone else in this world. A godly woman measures all her actions and words by them and strives to be an example of God's word. Not only will this godly woman have an excellent reputation, but the Christian community's reputation is also enhanced.

Our Legacy

It is not a bad thing to think about how the world remembers us after we die, even though our names are likely only to be remembered for a little while. However, our influence is still there.

> Many daughters have done well, but you excel them all. Charm is deceitful, and beauty is passing, but a woman who fears the Lord, she shall be praised. Give her of the fruit of her hands, and let her own works praise her in the gates (vv. 29-31).

King Lemmuel's mother probably taught him this description of the Proverbial woman to describe a worthy wife for her son. However, there are many real women included in the New Testament whose legacies are important to us today. Lydia worshipped with women at the riverbank in Philippi (Acts 16:11-15). Martha declared her belief that Jesus was Christ (John 11:27). Dorcas was full of good works and charitable deeds (Acts 9:36). Mary hosted a group praying for the release of Peter, who was in prison (Acts 12:12-17).

Personal Outlook and Our Reputations

Lesson 7

Remember the legacies of all the unnamed women in the New Testament! A woman with the issue of blood touched Jesus's hem because she believed He could heal her (Matt. 9: 20-22). The widow gave her two pennies into the temple offering, which was valued by Jesus more than the riches of others (Mark 12:41-44). Jesus blessed the Gentile woman who asked Him to heal her daughter because of her faith (Matt. 15:21-28).

What we do and who we are matters. It immediately matters to us and those in our families. However, our legacies can live forever! I am sure that Lydia was "just worshipping" on the Sabbath when her interaction with Paul lead to the salvation of her household. Martha was "just grieving" the death of her brother when she was one of the first to declare Jesus as Christ. Dorcas was "just sewing" clothes when she was helping others and demonstrating *agape* love. Mary was "just managing" her household as she raised John Mark to be a Christian leader.

Those unnamed women in the New Testament certainly did not consider themselves to be valuable, especially to those who live more than 2000 years later! However, their faith in God teaches us about living godly lives today.

The smallest stone makes a ripple in the pond. Each of us has an influence greater than we imagine. While we are on this earth, we are a living legacy just as these New Testament women.

Discussion Questions

1. Some descriptions in the Beatitudes seem to be a negative quality. Why are the following "blessed'?

    Poor in spirit

    Mourning

    Meek

    Hunger and thirst

2. How do these descriptions in the Beatitudes contribute to anyone's reputation?

    Merciful

    Pure in heart

    Peacemakers

3. Why and how do family dynamics influence a woman's reputation?

4. How does the way we speak affect our reputations?

5. How can a virtuous woman have a poor family reputation?

Personal Outlook and Our Reputations

Lesson 7

How can a woman destroy a good family reputation?

6. Is *agape* love important to a virtuous woman?

    How does *agape* love influence her reputation?

7. How does our reputation affect the church's reputation?

    Why does God care about either of these?

8. What are some ways to implement the commandments from Romans 12:9-21?

9. Is it vain to think about our legacies? Why or why not?

10. Name your Bible heroine. Why is she important to you?

Time Management

Chapter 8—Time Management

Time management is a common topic in the business world. Time is a limited resource for each person. It is also a hard topic as each person perceives time differently and approaches the activities of his or her day in many different ways.

How can time management become a woman's class subject from the description of the wife in Proverbs 31? The proverbial woman's productivity is proof of her excellent time management skills! Consider these verses and think of all she and her entire household accomplished each day. She planned her day from beginning to end!

She seeks wool and flax, and willingly works with her hands. She is like the merchant ships; she brings her food from afar. She also rises while it is yet night, and provides food for her household, And a portion for her maidservants. She considers a field and buys it; from her profits she plants a vineyard (vv. 13-16).

She perceives that her merchandise is good, and her lamp does not go out by night. She stretches out her hands to the distaff, and her hand holds the

Time Management

spindle. She extends her hand to the poor, yes, she reaches out her hands to the needy. She is not afraid of snow for her household, for all her household is clothed with scarlet. She makes tapestry for herself; her clothing is fine linen and purple (vv. 18-22).

She makes linen garments and sells them, and supplies sashes for the merchants (v. 25).

She watches over the ways of her household and does not eat the bread of idleness (v. 27).

Charm is deceitful and beauty is passing, but a woman who fears the Lord, she shall be praised. Give her of the fruit of her hands, and let her own works praise her in the gates. (vv. 30-31).

Is a planned day the goal for today's virtuous woman? Must we work our plan as soon as our feet hit the floor in the morning until we crawl back into bed at night? No, that is not the goal for a Christian and is not why we must think about time management. God does not mean for His people to be time driven. However, it is important to think about how we use our time.

Time is the one thing that is the same for every human—a second is a second; a minute is a minute; an hour is an hour. Once a second, minute, or an hour passes, it is gone and cannot be recovered. Every human has an unknown but finite amount of time allotted to them on earth.

In Ecclesiastes 3:1-8, Solomon writes about time. Solomon's words were rearranged and set into a popular 1960s song called "Turn, Turn, Turn" by Pete Seeger of the Byrds. Seeger's song is a plea for world peace, but is world peace what Solomon was teaching us about time?

Turn! Turn! Turn! By Pete Seeger
To everything There Is a Season—Words: Ecclesiastes 3:1-8

CHORUS:

           D   G   G/F#   Em7
To everything turn, turn, turn
                  D   G   G/F#   Em7
There is a season turn, turn, turn
       A7   D
And a time for every purpose, under heaven
          A7   D   A7   D
A time to be born, a time to die, a time to plant, a time to reap
         A7   D   G   (Bm)   A7   D
A time to kill, a time to heal, a time to laugh, a time to weep

CHORUS:
A time to build up, a time to break down
A time to dance, a time to mourn
A time to cast away stones, a time to gather stones together

CHORUS:
A time of love, a time of hate
A time of war, a time of peace
A time you may embrace, a time to refrain from embracing

CHORUS:
A time to gain, a time to lose
A time to rend, a time to sew
A time to love, a time to hate
A time for peace, I swear it's not too late

From www.traditionalmusic.co.uk

Solomon's biggest lesson to us about time is in the verses following the song.

> *What profit has the worker from that in which he labors? I have seen the God-given task with which the sons of men are to be occupied. He has made everything beautiful in its time. Also He has put eternity in their hearts, except that no one can find out the work that God does from beginning to end. I know that nothing is better for them than to rejoice, and to do good in their lives, and also that every man should eat and drink and enjoy the good of all his labor—it is the gift of God* (Eccles. 3:9-13).

Eternity in our hearts and enjoying God's gifts is what Solomon is teaching. We can rejoice here on earth and enjoy all the things for which we work, as there is a time and place for everything. However, God has put eternity in our

Time Management

Lesson 8

hearts; our souls strive to be with Him in eternity. That is the goal of our time and labor. Time management matters so much if we are to achieve this goal.

Planning for Eternity

We achieve eternity with God by making a life plan for ourselves following God's plan for salvation. Time management is required to reach the goals of our life plan. Jesus taught this as large crowds were with Him.

> *For which of you, intending to build a tower, does not sit down first and count the cost, whether he has enough to finish it—lest, after he has laid the foundation, and is not able to finish, all who see it begin to mock him, saying, "This man began to build and was not able to finish"? Or what king, going to make war against another king, does not sit down first and consider whether he is able with ten thousand to meet him who comes against him with twenty thousand? Or else, while the other is still a great way off, he sends a delegation and asks conditions of peace (Luke 14:28-32).*

Jesus knew that each person must deliberately choose and plan to follow Him. We cannot say "I am a follower of Jesus if we do not intentionally choose obedience to His teaching. This choice requires planning and management, as building a tower or defeating invaders does. These plans require a deliberate choice in the utilization of our time and resources.

One of the most uncertain stories in the Bible is Paul and Felix in Acts 24. Repeatedly Paul reasoned with Felix concerning faith in Christ. Felix's response was, "when I have a convenient time, I will call you." Felix did not use his time well in planning for his eternity. He let his hours, minutes, and seconds pass without following God's plan for our salvation.

> *And after some days, when Felix came with his wife Drusilla, who was Jewish, he sent for Paul and heard him concerning the faith in Christ. Now as he reasoned about righteousness, self-control, and the judgment to come, Felix was afraid and answered, "Go away for now; when I have a convenient time, I will call for you." Meanwhile, he also hoped that money would be given him by Paul, that he might release him. Therefore he sent for him more often and conversed with him (vv. 24-26).*

We must deliberately choose obedience to God's plan to find out if Felix ever chose obedience too! Felix allowed his anxiety about the future and the busyness of his life to delay his thoughts and deliberation to choose God's way.

The Proverbial Woman and Dwight Eisenhower

Consider the efforts of the proverbial woman. She sought, worked, and spun wool and flax. She acquired and prepared food. She bought a field and developed a vineyard. She sold garments, sashes, and other merchandise made by her household. She sewed tapestries and clothes. She supervised all the resources, work, and needs of all her household. She provided help and charity for the needy. Proverbs tells us that she started early and worked late and that her work was good and praiseworthy.

Verse 30 says, "But a woman who fears the Lord, she shall be praised." She feared and worshiped God. This was her most praiseworthy quality! All these activities weren't accidental; they were intentional, requiring planning for both her resources and her time. We today and the proverbial woman in Old Testament times are alike in that we all have the same number of minutes in each day.

Her time management supported her faith, her household, and her community. She had only so much time and resources and balanced the important and the urgent each day. To be successful, the proverbial woman must have used techniques made famous by Dwight Eisenhower. President Eisenhower said, "I have two kinds of problems: the urgent and the important. The urgent are not important, and the important are never urgent."

Important activities are those that help us to achieve our spiritual, personal, and professional goals. These activities consider long term goals and support those goals. Urgent activities require immediate attention and have immediate consequences because they are thrust upon us, such as a ringing phone, illness, or an accident. Urgent activities often get most of our attention and do not necessarily help us to achieve either our heavenly or our earthly goals. An Eisenhower matrix will help to demonstrate the difference in important and urgent activities.

Time Management

	Not Important	Important
URGENT	**Quadrant 1 (Manage)** Crisis and emergencies Sickness Last-minute preparations for scheduled activities Deadlines, ex, Tax Day Paying late bills	**Quadrant 2 (FOCUS)** Spiritual growth and service Important relationships Good health practices Big-picture planning for future Financial planning Scheduled activities Recreation, hobbies, rest
NOT URGENT	**Quadrant 3 (Avoid)** Trivial activities Some calls, emails, texts, shopping Time wasters, such as mindless web surfing Social media without a purpose Watching TV or video games for hours Perfectionism Escape activities—procrastination	**Quadrant 4 (Minimize)** Interruptions Some calls, emails, texts, spam Some meetings, invitations, and obligations Some shopping Shallow relationships

    Our goal is to spend the most time in Quadrant 2. This quadrant is where our long-term goals are established, planned, and achieved. As today's virtuous women, we must prioritize our spiritual needs versus our earthly ones to achieve the "eternity in our hearts." This prioritization is like making a "heavenly versus earthly" Eisenhower sub-chart within our Quadrant 2! *Focusing* on Quadrant 2 is how we achieve both our earthly and heavenly goals.

    When you are considering your Quadrant 2 activities for your "heavenly versus earthly" sub-chart, weigh your accomplishments to your time with God. Many great earthly activities may be too important and become a stumbling block to achieving your eternity with God. Remember, the proverbial woman's greatest achievement was *fearing the Lord* even though she had an enviable list of accomplishments. Also, remember that she did not achieve all those accomplishments in one day. She was like the king who was considering making war in Luke 14. She planned and counted the cost.

    If you are always putting out fires and stressed to the max, then you are spending too much time in Quadrant 1. It is okay not to answer every email, phone call, or volunteer request. Your ally to prevent burn-out is more time in Quadrant 2. Planning how you want to use your time and resources helps you to know how to manage the urgent problems. More thinking and planning prevent the stress and burn-out of crisis management in Quadrant 1. Improved time *management* is the best way to control Quadrant 1.

Too much time in Quadrant 3 results in victimization, lack of control, purpose, or planning. This quadrant is like the "wide gate" leading to destruction in Matthew 7:13. Going with the flow through the wide gate is easy when a person has not decided to achieve the "eternity in his heart." Time spent in this quadrant has no valuable results for any goal. The best strategy to control Quadrant 3 is to avoid spending time in the quadrant.

Irresponsibility and procrastination are good descriptions for too much time in Quadrant 4. The motto of this quadrant is, "I'm going to get around to it." This quadrant may be the easiest one in which to stay, and perhaps the most pleasant. In this quadrant, people float along, minding their own business, achieving nothing. However, this person knows what the important activities are just as the rich, young ruler did (Mark 10:17-22). This young man knew what Jesus told him to do for eternal life and chose not to do it. *Minimize the time in Quadrant 4.*

Mary and Martha

Mary and Martha are good examples to illustrate urgent and important activities.

Now it happened as they went that He entered a certain village, and a certain woman named Martha welcomed Him into her house. And she had a sister called Mary, who also sat at Jesus' feet and heard His word. But Martha was distracted with much serving, and she approached Him and said, "Lord, do You not care that my sister has left me to serve alone? Therefore tell her to help me." And Jesus answered and said to her, "Martha, Martha, you are worried and troubled about many things. But one thing is needed, and Mary has chosen that good part, which will not be taken away from her" (Luke 10:38-42).

Hospitality was very significant, almost sacred, during Bible times. Mary and Martha extended love and friendship when they provided a meal for Jesus. Martha is very concerned with the urgent matters of serving her guests and meeting the high expectations of her culture.

The above verses tell us that Martha welcomed Jesus into her house but becomes indignant with Mary for not helping with the serving. Mary had chosen to listen to Jesus's teaching. Martha was totally in Quadrant 1 as she handled the preparation and set up of a meal for Jesus and His followers. Mary was dwelling in Quadrant 2 as she fed the eternity in her heart with the teaching of Jesus.

Jesus recognizes this in his reply to Martha. "Martha, Martha, you are worried and troubled about many things. But one thing is needed, and Mary has chosen that good part, which will not be taken away from her."

Sometimes it is hard to choose spiritual matters in Quadrant 2 when everything seems to scream urgency in Quadrant 1. Each of us must learn to recognize what is important and leads us to eternity as we choose how to spend our time.

Are We Lazy or Are We Resting?

The Bible has many warnings against laziness, especially in Proverbs. God has never wanted His people to be slothful. He always wants His people to be productive in both earthly and spiritual matters.

> Go to the ant, you sluggard! Consider her ways and be wise, Which, having no captain, Overseer or ruler, Provides her supplies in the summer, And gathers her food in the harvest. How long will you slumber, O sluggard? When will you rise from your sleep? A little sleep, a little slumber, A little folding of the hands to sleep—So shall your poverty come on you like a prowler, And your need like an armed man *(Prov. 6:6-11).*

TODAY'S VIRTUOUS WOMAN

Aesop's fable about the ant and the grasshopper echoes the lesson of these verses. Neither the sluggard nor the grasshopper makes plans which use their time well. They are wasting their opportunities and their time. Opportunities may occur again, but the time is gone forever.

God knows that His people need rest. Heaven is often described as a place of rest. Jesus and His apostles rested in Mark 6. It is important to note that Jesus and His apostles had worked very hard to teach others, were tired due to this work, and needed rest because of this work.

> Then the apostles gathered to Jesus and told Him all things, both what they had done and what they had taught. And He said to them, "Come aside by yourselves to a deserted place and rest a while." For there were many coming and going, and they did not even have time to eat. So they departed to a deserted place in the boat by themselves (Mark 6:30-32).

God knows that we need to rest when we are mentally and physically tired. However, He desires for His people to be productive—to use their time well.

> For you yourselves know how you ought to follow us, for we were not disorderly among you; nor did we eat anyone's bread free of charge, but worked with labor and toil night and day, that we might not be a burden to any of you, not because we do not have authority, but to make ourselves an example of how you should follow us. For even when we were with you, we commanded you this: If anyone will not work, neither shall he eat. For we hear that there are some who walk among you in a disorderly manner, not working at all, but are busybodies. Now those who are such

Time Management

we command and exhort through our Lord Jesus Christ that they work in quietness and eat their own bread (2 Thess. 3:7-12).

God also knows that each of us doesn't have the same opportunities or capabilities. This is apparent from Matthew 25, where Jesus teaches in the parable of the talents:

For the kingdom of heaven is like a man traveling to a far country, who called his own servants and delivered his goods to them. And to one he gave five talents, to another two, and to another one, to each according to his own ability; and immediately he went on a journey (vv. 14-15).

The master knew each servant's ability. God knows our abilities too! The master expected each servant to use his talents to the best of his ability—working for the good of the master. In the following verses, the master punishes the servant who did not work for the master and gave more to his profitable servants. The proverbial woman used her opportunities, resources, and abilities well. We must also use ours well, as we work in the Lord's kingdom.

We Plan, God Wills

So, today's virtuous woman wants to please God and has developed excellent time management skills, which emphasize Quadrant 2. Has she pleased God?

Come now, you who say, "Today or tomorrow we will go to such and such a city, spend a year there, buy and sell, and make a profit"; whereas you do not know what will happen tomorrow. For what is your life? It is even a vapor that appears for a little time and then vanishes away. Instead, you ought to say, "If the Lord wills, we shall live and do this or that." But now you boast in your arrogance. All such boasting is evil (Jas. 4:13-16).

"If the Lord wills." These words must have precedence in all our planning. Life is uncertain. None of us know what the future will bring. As we travel, buy and sell, and build our profitable businesses, it is so important that God has the highest priority in our life. When God is our goal and our compass, then the Lord's will is part of all our plans. Today's virtuous woman knows that God's will is the only will of importance and considers His will in all her decisions and planning. She may make her plans, but God makes things happen: "A man's heart plans his way, But the Lord directs his steps" (Prov. 16:9).

Do What Glorifies God

The proverbial woman is a wonderful example of someone whose works glorified God. Proverbs 31 describes so many of her accomplishments; however, her greatest accomplishment is described last: "A woman who fears the Lord, she shall be praised" (Prov. 31:30).

Praise for a woman who fears the Lord? Is that a goal? In today's culture, this is often not a praiseworthy goal. Women are taught to be self-sufficient and to strive for earthly rewards. Earthly rewards are not eternal rewards, are not what God wants, and do not glorify Him. God wants our hearts and our commitment to Him. He has given us a lot of direction to live a Christian life.

> *But concerning brotherly love you have no need that I should write to you, for you yourselves are taught by God to love one another; and indeed you do so toward all the brethren who are in all Macedonia. But we urge you, brethren, that you increase more and more; that you also aspire to lead a quiet life, to mind your own business, and to work with your own hands, as we commanded you, that you may walk properly toward those who are outside, and that you may lack nothing* (1 Thess. 4:9-12).

God wants today's virtuous women to manage the time that He gives us and to remember that He is first in our lives. Our lives should reflect God and His goodness. Remember, we can plan, but those plans happen "if the Lord wills."

Discussion Questions

1. How is time management a relevant subject based on the woman in Proverbs 31?

2. Is the "eternity in our hearts" of Ecclesiastes 3:11 relevant to how we use our time? If yes, then how is it relevant?

3. Why do we need to plan for eternity? How are these plans part of our daily life?

Time Management

4. Build an Eisenhower matrix for your life.

	Not Important	Important
URGENT	Quadrant 1 (Manage)	Quadrant 2 (FOCUS)
NOT URGENT	Quadrant 3 (Avoid)	Quadrant 4 (Minimize)

Would a Quadrant 2 sub-chart of heavenly versus earthly be helpful to you?

5. What changes would you like to see in your matrix? Are these changes important to a Christian?

6. Was Martha sinful when she was concerned with serving her guests? Why or why not?

7. How do we know if we are being lazy or enjoying a needed rest?

8. Can our hobbies and recreation become a problem as we strive to achieve "eternity'?

9. How does "If the Lord wills," affect your planning?

How do our daily lives glorify God?

Beauty and Fashion

Chapter 9—Beauty and Fashion

In the beginning . . . God made . . . man and woman . . . and indeed it was very good (Genesis 1:1-31).

Have you ever wondered why God made a woman with physical beauty and then made her beauty an issue to righteousness? God made Eve and said it was good—beauty and all. God's creation is not the question. The real question is how a woman views her beauty and what she does with it.

Beautiful People in the Bible

The Bible tells us of beautiful people—both men and women. Their beauty was part of who they were. Our beauty or handsomeness is part of us.

- *Saul*—He had a choice and handsome son whose name was Saul. There was not a more handsome person than he among the children of Israel. From his shoulders upward, he was taller than any of the people (1 Sam. 9:2).
- *David*—Now he was ruddy, with bright eyes, and good-looking (1 Sam. 16:12b).
- *Sarai*—You are a woman of beautiful countenance (Gen. 12:11b).
- *Rebekah*—Now the young woman was very beautiful to behold (Gen. 24:16a).
- *Rachel*—Rachel was beautiful of form and appearance (Gen. 29:17b).
- *Bathsheba*—The woman was very beautiful to behold (2 Sam. 11:2b).

- ***Abigail**—She was a woman of good understanding and beautiful appearance* (1 Sam. 25:3b).

- ***Esther**—The young woman was lovely and beautiful* (Esth. 2:7b).

Sometimes, God chooses to tell us that certain people are beautiful when He is making a point. For instance, Saul was a particularly handsome man and made a regal-looking king. He was everything that the Israelites thought a king should be and was the people's choice. However, he was not a good king, nor was he faithful to God. Saul was not beautiful on the inside.

On the other hand, David was Jesse's youngest son and a shepherd. As such, he was not destined to be the leader of his clan, much less a nation. Samuel himself would have chosen one of David's brothers: "But the Lord said to Samuel, 'Do not look at his appearance or at his physical stature, because I have refused him. For the Lord does not see as man sees; for man looks at the outward appearance, but the Lord looks at the heart'" (1 Sam. 16:6-13). God valued David's inner qualities more than his outward appearance. The Bible tells us that David was a man of God's own heart who obeyed God's will (Acts 13:22). This inner quality is the true beauty that God values.

Abigail was beautiful and *smart*. She prevented David and his men from destroying Nabal and the whole shearing camp. Yet, as she interceded for noxious Nabal and averted David's sinful raid, Abigail used her brains, not her beauty. The Bible praises Abigail, not her attractiveness, but for her actions

Beautiful Vashti is the Persian queen whose story is in Esther 1. While King Ahasuerus gave a seven-day feast for the visiting male rulers, she was hosting a feast for their women. After seven drunken days, the king commanded the presence of Vashti to show off her beauty. Vashti refused to come before all the intoxicated men. The men did not want their women to be disobedient to their commands as Vashti was to Ahasuerus's command and advised the king to remove her as queen—which he did. The story moves on to Esther and Mordecai; however, beautiful Vashti displays commendable inner qualities. She was supportive of her husband, as is evident by her refusal to participate in a vulgar display for inebriated men. She stood up for what was right, even when she knew there would be a price to pay. We should praise Vashti's inner qualities. Instead, she is the forgettable character in the book of Esther.

Our Beauty

Very few women are confident in their beauty. Most of us are critical of ourselves and do not see our beauty as God sees it. When we are young, we

Beauty and Fashion

want to be as beautiful as actresses and models. As we age, we worry about creeping weight and wrinkles. When measured by worldly standards, we often don't measure up. Those standards are artificial and change over time! For example, women with the palest complexions were beautiful in the 1800s, but by the late 1900s, sun-kissed skin was more valued. Skin did not change over those decades, but our cosmetic view of the skin did change.

God made our outside appearance. And yes, some of us are prettier than others. Nevertheless, God places more value on our hearts. What do we treasure in our hearts? What is the center of our consciousness? God looks at our hearts to see the "real" person, not merely the outward appearance that others see.

Know the God of your father, and serve Him with a loyal heart and with a willing mind; for the Lord searches all hearts and understands all the intent of the thoughts. If you seek Him, He will be found by you; but if you forsake Him, He will cast you off forever (1 Chron. 28:9).

The above verse is David's advice to his son, Solomon. David knew that it was more important for his son to pursue God than earthly aspirations. It was essential for Solomon to have a heart for God rather than all his riches, beauty, wisdom, or any other worldly ambitions. It took Solomon all his life to come to the same conclusion. After Solomon spends his life pursuing earthly goals, he realizes in Ecclesiastes 12.

> Let us hear the conclusion of the whole matter: Fear God and keep His commandments, for this is man's all. For God will bring every work into judgment, including every secret thing, whether good or evil *(Eccles. 12:13-14).*

Today, we can live by David's advice to pursue God, instead of delaying like Solomon. God looks at the beauty of our hearts and not the beauty of our bodies.

Sinful Beauty

We can trust in our beauty and use it sinfully. Sinful use of beauty happens when we forget that all we have is a gift from God and trust in our earthly beauty to keep us safe and secure. Ezekiel compared Jerusalem to such a woman.

> But you trusted in your own beauty, played the harlot because of your fame, and poured out your harlotry on everyone passing by who would have it... You built your high places at the head of every road, and made your beauty to be abhorred *(Ezek. 16: 15, 25).*

Proverbs has many warnings about sinful beauty. Beauty can be used to flatter and seduce to obtain worldly advantages. Beautiful women are often compared to prostitutes in the book of Proverbs, which is unfortunate for us women. However, that tells us how easily beauty is used sinfully.

> To keep you from the evil woman, from the flattering tongue of a seductress. Do not lust after her beauty in your heart, nor let her allure you with her eyelids. For by means of a harlot a man is reduced to a crust of bread; and an adulteress will prey upon his precious life *(Prov. 6:24-26).*

The beauty of our hearts is so much more important than any outward beauty. Our outward appearance should always reflect what is in our hearts. If we appear "saintly" on the outside and only think of evil in our hearts, we are like the lovely woman in Proverbs 11. Her outside appearance had as much value as a gold ring in a pig's nose!

> As a ring of gold in a swine's snout, so is a lovely woman who lacks discretion *(Prov. 11:22).*

The Bible reveals that beauty has caused sin. David lusted after beautiful Bathsheba as she bathed. This sinful lust led to adultery and murder. Abram lied to protect himself when Pharaoh wanted beautiful Sarai for a wife. Matthew 5:28 warns that looking lustfully at a woman is mentally committing adultery.

Beauty and Fashion

But I say to you that whoever looks at a woman to lust for her has already committed adultery with her in his heart (Matt. 5:28).

Knowing that your beauty can cause another to sin is an unwelcome burden for all women. Certainly, neither Bathsheba nor Sarai wanted David or Abram to sin because of their beauty. However, today's virtuous woman must be aware of this burden, and most sermons on modesty prioritize this idea. Modest women can always debate whether they are the cause of someone else's sin. Still, a virtuous woman must be aware of this problem so that they are not necessarily a stumbling block for another person. 1 Corinthians 10:31 can also be applied in our manner of dress. "Therefore, whether you eat or drink, or whatever you do, do all to the glory of God." Our clothing must also reflect God's glory.

Value of Beauty and Fashion

The proverbial woman was fashionable. After all, the proverbial woman wore colorful and fine linen clothes. Scarlet and purple dyes were costly in Old Testament times, and both she and her household wore scarlet and purple clothes. Christians can also wear colorful and attractive clothes as drab and dull fashion does not add to anyone's heart. The important qualities of her beauty were her inner qualities. Our clothes can be attractive and not draw undue or wrong attention to our bodies.

She is not afraid of snow for her household, for all her household is clothed with scarlet. She makes tapestry for herself; her clothing is fine linen and purple (vv. 21-22).

She makes linen garments and sells them, and supplies sashes for the merchants. Strength and honor are her clothing; she shall rejoice in time to come (vv. 24-25).

Charm is deceitful and beauty is passing, but a woman who fears the Lord, she shall be praised (v. 30).

Christians are not taught to avoid fashion. However, how we dress is important. We must be choosy in our fashion. Your beauty should be based on your internal values and not on outside appearance. We cannot wear immodest clothing to look like worldly people and not be influenced by them or influence those with whom we come into contact. Good taste should always prevail for our clothes, and our best ornamentation should be what is in our hearts.

Do not let your adornment be merely outward—arranging the hair, wearing gold, or putting on fine apparel—rather let it be the hidden person of the heart, with the incorruptible beauty of a gentle and quiet spirit, which is very precious in the sight of God. For in this manner, in former times, the holy women who trusted in God also adorned themselves, being submissive to their own husbands, as Sarah obeyed Abraham, calling him lord, whose daughters you are if you do good and are not afraid with any terror (1 Pet. 3:3-6).

1 Peter 3 does not picture today's current fashion, which shows a lot of skin and is very body-conscious. Contemporary fashion is designed to cause others to specifically notice a person's body, not anything about the inner qualities of that person. It is more like the difference in Saul and David's appearance related to being chosen as king. Modern fashion appeals to Saul-followers who look for earthly measures for beauty. A Christian should dress in fashions that follow "God's own heart" and adorn themselves with things that are precious to God, as David did.

Wearing godly fashion does not require head-to-toe shapeless clothing, such as a burka. Excessively drab clothing may also be a vanity. Trying to be the least stylishly dressed woman may be as prideful as another extreme. However, a godly woman does wear modest clothing. 1 Timothy 2:9 stresses modesty, propriety, and moderation: "in like manner also, that the women adorn themselves in modest apparel, with propriety and moderation, not with braided hair or gold or pearls or costly clothing."

Beauty and Fashion

Notice both 1 Timothy 2:9 and 1 Peter 3:3 mention costly apparel, fancy hairdos, and jewelry. Does this teach us to avoid costly apparel, fancy hairdos, and jewelry? No, that isn't the point in the verses. Peter said, "Do not let your adornment be merely outward . . . rather let it be the hidden person of the heart, with the incorruptible beauty of a gentle and quiet spirit, which is very precious in the sight of God" (1 Pet. 3:3-4). God does not want our beauty only to be what we wear and how we style our hair. The beauty and fashion that God desires are the qualities of our hearts. He wants those qualities to be what shines from us and not our "golden" fashion. God wants us to dress as did Job: "I put on righteousness, and it clothed me; My justice was like a robe and a turban" (Job 29:14).

If righteousness, strength, and honor describe your outfit for the day or an event, then that outfit would be approved by God as Job was right. Remember the verse describing the beauty of the proverbial woman: "Charm is deceitful and beauty is passing, but a woman who fears the Lord, she shall be praised" (v. 30).

Fashion during Worship

Recently my daughter-in-law asked me where the Bible told us to dress up for Sunday worship. She had diligently searched and had not found any verses for this practice. She felt that "out of respect for God" that all worshippers should wear their "Sunday best" and did just that. Is wearing our "Sunday best" to worship a commandment from God or a tradition from man? After all, most people had one change of clothes in Bible times.

Usually, Christians are advised not to appear proud or not to act like they are better than someone else. For example, in Luke 20, Jesus condemns the scribes for their dress. The scribes used their clothes to distinguish themselves as superior from other people.

> *Beware of the scribes, who desire to go around in long robes, love greetings in the marketplaces, the best seats in the synagogues, and the best places at feasts, who devour widows' houses, and for a pretense make long prayers. These will receive greater condemnation* (Luke 20:46-47).

So, is dressing in our better clothes for weekly worship something that the Bible tells us to do, or does it tell us to avoid this practice? God wants us to dress appropriately for worship and tells us so in Matthew 22.

> *And Jesus answered and spoke to them again by parables and said: "The kingdom of heaven is like a certain king who arranged a marriage for his son, and sent out his servants to call those who were invited to the wedding; and they were not willing to come. Again, he sent out other servants, saying, 'Tell those who are invited, 'See, I have prepared my dinner; my oxen and fatted cattle are killed, and all things are ready. Come to the wedding." But they made light of it and went their ways, one to his own farm, another to his business. And the rest seized his servants, treated them spitefully, and killed them. But when the king heard about it, he was furious. And he sent out his armies, destroyed those murderers, and burned up their city. Then he said to his servants, 'The wedding is ready, but those who were invited were not worthy. Therefore go into the highways, and as many as you find, invite to the wedding.' So those servants went out into the highways and gathered together all whom they found, both bad and good. And the wedding hall was filled with guests. But when the king came in to see the guests, he saw a man there who did not have on a wedding garment. So he said to him, 'Friend, how did you come in here without a wedding garment?' And he was speechless. Then the king said to the servants, 'Bind him hand and foot, take him away, and cast him into outer darkness; there will be weeping and gnashing of teeth'"* (Matt. 22:1-13).

There is plenty to study in this parable! Often, when this parable is studied, the gospel for the Gentiles is the usual discussion. However, the relevant part for this parable for fashion during worship is in verses 11 through 13. At this time, the wedding guests have been found on the highways and were both good and bad people. They would not all have had nice clothes for the wedding.

Still, the master expected the guests to dress for the wedding feast to show appropriate respect for the host. All the guests were expected to have cleaned up for the wedding. The poorest with no other outfit would have washed and straightened their clothes as best as they could. Others with better clothes

Beauty and Fashion

wore those better clothes for the wedding. In verse 11, by not dressing properly for the wedding, the guest did not honor the master and was thus rejected.

God expects us to show similar respect during worship today. All worshippers will not have the same money to spend on clothes, and God knows this. However, God expects us to be wearing our "wedding" clothes and to show Him proper respect during our worship. During the Old Testament times, God expected the best of the flocks and fields to be His offerings from the Israelites. He doesn't expect less from us today.

Clothes to Desire

Let's conclude our lesson on fashion and beauty with a discussion about the clothing that God desires for us—the whole armor of God.

Therefore take up the whole armor of God, that you may be able to withstand in the evil day, and having done all, to stand. Stand therefore, having girded your waist with truth, having put on the breastplate of righteousness, and having shod your feet with the preparation of the gospel of peace; above all, taking the shield of faith with which you will be able to quench all the fiery darts of the wicked one. And take the helmet of salvation, and the sword of the Spirit, which is the word of God; praying always with all prayer and supplication in the Spirit, being watchful to this end with all perseverance and supplication for all the saints (Eph. 6:13-18).

Gird your waist with truth—Roman soldiers wore a belt from which hung pieces of leather to protect them. Christians are protected by the truth, which is the word of God, and by their integrity and honesty.

The breastplate of righteousness—By Webster's definition, righteousness is "acting in accord with divine or moral law: free from guilt or sin." For a Christian, righteousness is obedience to God for all His commandments are righteousness (Ps. 119:172). Righteousness protects all those who wear it just as the breastplate protected the soldier. It is important to notice that righteousness requires action from a Christian to obey God's commandments. We must put on our righteousness as the Roman soldier put on his breastplate. Our righteousness guards our hearts, just like the breastplate guarded the soldier's heart.

Shod your feet with the preparation of the gospel of peace—Roman soldiers wore spiked sandals, which were innovative technology for the time. The spikes helped the soldier to stand firm in a slippery battlefield and to keep traction while marching. Christians need both characteristics. The gospel of peace is a firm foundation on which the Christian stands. The Christian soldier also needs to be ready to march on to defend and spread the gospel of peace. This readiness requires time spent with God and in the word of God.

The shield of faith—A Roman soldier's shield protected all or part of his body at any time. Remember the movies where the soldiers stand under their shields as fiery arrows shoot from the enemy lines? The shield repeals the fiery arrows, so the soldiers are not hurt unless uncovered by the shield. A Christian's faith is their shield. A properly utilized "shield of faith" will protect a Christian from the fiery arrows of Satan.

The helmet of salvation—A helmet is worn on and protects the head. The head is where a Christian considers and deliberates the word of God to thoughtfully gain the wisdom that leads to salvation (2 Tim. 3:15). This careful consideration becomes the helmet of salvation for today's virtuous woman.

The sword of the spirit is the word of God—This sword is the only offensive weapon mentioned in the armor of God. To use this offensive weapon means that the Christian *knows* the word of God. A Christian cannot have the words ready to teach anyone else unless they know the word of God themselves. All soldiers practice using a sword effectively. Similarly, a Christian must spend time in the word of God to be able to use it effectively.

Roman soldiers would never consider going into battle without his armor. Neither would they skip practice with their shield and sword. A Christian must daily use the armor of God in their lives as well. This armor is always the highest fashion!

Beauty and Fashion

Discussion Questions

1. Is beauty sinful? Why or why not?

2. How did the looks of Saul and David affect their relationship with God and their relationship with the Israelites?

3. Why does God value our hearts more than our beauty?

4. Why do women worry about their beauty?

5. How can a woman's beauty be a stumbling block?

6. Can a woman dress however she wants? Why or why not?

7. How can a virtuous woman dress fashionably?

8. Does God expect better outfits for Sunday worship? Justify your answer.

9. How can a woman wear the whole armor of God?

10. Is beauty only an issue for women? Why or why not?

Wise Words

Lesson 10—Wise Words

She opens her mouth with wisdom, and on her tongue is the law of kindness (Prov. 31:26).

Proverbs 31 tells us that the proverbial woman understood the power of words and controlled her tongue well. Our tongue is a small muscle weighing about two ounces. Even though this muscle is so small, it is powerful and is very hard to control. For this reason, lessons about the tongue usually discuss the negative aspects of the tongue. Let's start our discussion there and then move to the words of wisdom and kindness exhibited by the proverbial woman.

Even so the tongue is a little member and boasts great things. See how great a forest a little fire kindles! And the tongue is a fire, a world of iniquity. The tongue is so set among our members that it defiles the whole body, and sets on fire the course of nature; and it is set on fire by hell. For every kind of beast and bird, of reptile and creature of the sea, is tamed and has

Wise Words

been tamed by mankind. But no man can tame the tongue. It is an unruly evil, full of deadly poison. With it we bless our God and Father, and with it we curse men, who have been made in the similitude of God. Out of the same mouth proceed blessing and cursing. My brethren, these things ought not to be so. Does a spring send forth fresh water and bitter from the same opening? Can a fig tree, my brethren, bear olives, or a grapevine bear figs? Thus no spring yields both salt water and fresh (Jas. 3:5-12).

The short book of James has only five chapters with instructions for the individual Christian. Of these five chapters, all of chapter three deals with controlling the tongue! James tells us that a foul tongue defiles the whole body! James is teaching that it is a Christian's priority to control her speech as speech is the window of the heart.

In verse 11, James tells us that a spring cannot have both fresh and bitter water. Our words reflect our thoughts and what is in our hearts. Our thoughts can be evil or good, and our tongue expresses those thoughts. When our words are as bitter water, Christian ideals of love, honesty, and compassion are nonexistent. A person listening to bitter words hears curses, evil, and worldly ideas. A Christian who speaks with "pure water" is controlling her tongue and has words of blessing which exhibit characteristics of Jesus's teaching.

James also tells us that it is hard to control our tongues. " But no man can tame the tongue. It is an unruly evil, full of deadly poison" (3:8). James had already offered sage advice about controlling our tongues in chapter one: "So then, my beloved brethren, let every man be swift to hear, slow to speak, slow to wrath" (1:9). James advises us to listen well, but be slow to respond with our words and to be slow to become angry. He knew that angry words could light the fires mentioned in verse 5 above.

Solomon had similar advice for us. "He who answers a matter before he hears it, it is folly and shame to him" (Prov. 18:13). Sometimes we are thinking of our response before the speaker has finished speaking. Thinking of our response is not listening at all! Yes, our ears capture the sound vibrations, and we have heard the sound; however, we have not listened to the words at all. How can our response begin to address the words of the speaker when we have not listened to his or her words?

Just a few evil or angry words can cause so much irreparable harm. All of us remember such words spoken to us by those whom we love or respect. Sometimes those angry words come to our memories before remembering kind words. I recall a few times that I lost my temper and spoke rashly. No good results came from those conversations, and the listeners of those words will remember how this Christian spoke to them in a very unkind manner. Speaking in anger is not the example that Jesus wanted when He told us to be the light on the lampstand giving light to all.

Divisive Words

An uncontrolled tongue is divisive and leads to quarrels. "The beginning of strife is like releasing water; therefore, stop contention before a quarrel starts" (Prov. 17:14). It takes two to quarrel, and one individual can stop a quarrel. Quarrels can cause deep divisions among family and friends. Evil persons use words to enhance their agendas and lead others into sin.

> *An ungodly man digs up evil, And it is on his lips like a burning fire. A perverse man sows strife, And a whisperer separates the best of friends. A violent man entices his neighbor and leads him in a way that is not good. He winks his eye to devise perverse things; He purses his lips and brings about evil* (Prov. 16:27-30).

There are three types of evil men in these verses, and all of them are using words for divisive purposes. In verse 27, the ungodly man gossips and looks for any bad thing about which to talk. He uses bad information purposely for evil, and his evil words spread like fire throughout his community. In verse 28, the perverse man starts a fight among friends. He whispers words in secret, but the words explode among the friends who cannot remain friends after the strife. In verse 29-30, the violent man persuades his neighbor to join him in his evil ways. His words make sin look more enticing than a godly life.

Words can cause gashes among friends and family. Unfortunately, most of us know situations where a quarrel created a gulf within our church family. This gulf can lead some Christians into sin and cause a division in the Lord's church. Words matter. Choose them carefully.

Secret Words

There is nothing sinful about secret words of themselves. All of us have confidants with whom we reveal our innermost thoughts and ideas. Sometimes these secret words are how we work out a problem. Sometimes these secret words are new ideas or projects for us or others. Such secret words are spoken in confidence and not for evil purposes. The type of secret words to be discussed here are those spoken slyly to influence the listener into wickedness and those repeated by the listener for malicious purposes.

Sly words are those spoken to sway the listener and to manipulate their thoughts or actions. These sly words often contain flattery or threats. This use of words is like the men mentioned in Proverbs 16:27-30 above who used words to

Wise Words

separate friends or entice the listener into iniquity. This speaker is purposely using secret words to cause another to think or act evilly and carry out wrongdoing.

Those who do wickedly against the covenant he shall corrupt with flattery, but the people who know their God shall be strong, and carry out great exploits (Dan. 11:32).

There is power in knowing the secrets of others. Our confidant may be a talebearer and use our secret words for their advantage or to make themselves more important. Proverbs 11:13a cautions us that "a talebearer reveals secrets." Solomon warns us again, "He who goes about as a talebearer reveals secrets; therefore do not associate with one who flatters with his lips" (Prov. 20:19). In this instance, the sin belongs to the talebearer, who is betraying the confidence of another. On the other hand, all of us must consider what we tell or confess to other people to prevent our secret words from being repeated by a talebearer.

Solomon also alerts us about listening to a talebearer: "The words of a talebearer are like tasty trifles, and they go down into the inmost body" (Prov. 18:8). This alert is so important that he repeats it almost verbatim in Proverbs 26:22. Many people have a ravenous appetite for tasty morsels of gossip about other people and actively seek relationships with talebearers. Rumors, gossip, and scandal are the highlights of their day. God does not want us to desire bad things for other people, but good things. Jesus's golden rule is a great example of God's desire. "Therefore, whatever you want men to do to you, do also to them, for this is the Law and the Prophets" (Matt. 7:12).

Slanderous Words

Slanderous and libelous words are those designed to insult, malign, vilify, or smear another person's reputation. Our legal system defines slander as the action or crime of making a false spoken statement damaging to a person's reputation and libel as written defamation. These words are lies mixed with enough truth to be believable. Speakers often disguise slander in politically correct speech or sound bites, telling only part of the truth.

David suffered from slander during his days of hiding in the wilderness and from his own family. His words of sorrow cry out to us in his psalms. Slanderous words alleged that David sought to overthrow King Saul and later that David was a poor king. This slander was not limited to David's enemies, but also by his family members.

> *For I hear the slander of many; Fear is on every side; While they take counsel together against me, They scheme to take away my life* (Ps. 31:13).

> *Whoever secretly slanders his neighbor, Him I will destroy; The one who has a haughty look and a proud heart, Him I will not endure* (Ps. 101:5).

> *Let not a slanderer be established in the earth; Let evil hunt the violent man to overthrow him"* (Ps. 140:11).

As we learn from Paul's warning in 2 Timothy 3, slanderers do not love God. Christians must turn away from slanderers.

> *For men will be lovers of themselves, lovers of money, boasters, proud, blasphemers, disobedient to parents, unthankful, unholy, unloving, unforgiving, slanderers, without self-control, brutal, despisers of good, traitors, headstrong, haughty, lovers of pleasure rather than lovers of God, having a form of godliness but denying its power. And from such people turn away!* (vv. 2-5).

Paul specifically warns women about slander: "the older women likewise, that they be reverent in behavior, not slanderers, not given to much wine,

Wise Words

teachers of good things" (Titus 2:3), Again, in 1 Timothy 3:11, the wives of deacons are not to be slanderers. Slander is such an evil thing that God does not want it in His church. Sometimes idleness nurtures gossip and slander. Paul warns younger widows about that also: "And besides, they learn to be idle, wandering about from house to house, and not only idle but also gossips and busybodies, saying things which they ought not" (1 Tim. 5:13).

Slander is dangerous words intending unkind, malicious, vindictive, or harsh outcomes for the targeted person(s). Repeating slanderous words against a person is the same as initiating that slander. Know the truth before you speak!

Contentious Words

Contention is a heated disagreement leading to conflict between individuals and groups. Wise Solomon cautions us about contentious words: "A fool's lips enter into contention, and his mouth calls for blows" (Prov. 18:6). We can disagree with someone without causing contention. Reason flees when anger enters a disagreement, and victory becomes the prize, not harmony.

Korah and his allies created conflict among the Israelites with their contentious words (Num. 16:1-35). Korah desired a more prestigious leadership role among the priests and persuaded 250 leaders of the congregation to rebel against Moses's leadership. Korah's words convinced these men who knew that Moses was God's chosen leader to defy Moses's guidance. Korah accused Moses of exalting himself over all the Israelite people. Korah was ready for a fight just as Solomon warns in Proverbs 18:6.

Do you remember the rest of the store? God destroyed Korah and all his followers, along with their families and possessions. Korah's contentious words resulted in death for many innocent people. Our contentious words can have a similar result today. Hear Solomon's best advice in this situation: "Therefore, stop contention before a quarrel starts" (Prov. 17:14b).

Deceitful Words

The person speaking deceitful words is never desiring good for the listener, but only for herself. Deceit and trickery can hide a small injustice or cause great sin.

People do not believe known deceivers even when they tell the truth. The story of the young shepherd crying "Wolf" portrays this situation. This boy was supposed to watch the sheep and call "Wolf" when danger threatened the sheep. He falsely called for help so many times that when real peril threatened and he cried "Wolf," no help came.

People deceive and lie for all kinds of reasons. Jealousy, hatred, and self-promotion often top the list. Liars frequently believe their lies! Remember this proverbial advice: "He who hates disguises it with his lips, and lays up deceit within himself; when he speaks kindly, do not believe him" (Prov. 26:24-25). Do not necessarily believe kind words from a liar. Duplicity and self-promotion are probably the goal and not real kindness. Proverbs 29:5 teaches us that "a man who flatters his neighbor spreads a net for his feet."

The Gibeonites deceived the Israelites into disobeying God (Josh. 9:3-27). The people of Gibeon were Hivites, lived about five miles northwest of Jerusalem, and listed for destruction in Exodus 34:11. God did not want Israel to become allies with pagan nations of Canaan. However, the Gibeonites went to great lengths to appear to be from a faraway country, and Israel could make treaties from faraway lands (Exod. 34:11, 12; Deut. 20:10-18). The Gibeonites' deceitful words and worn-out possessions rang true to the ears of Joshua and the Israelites, who did not seek the counsel of God. So, the Israelites and a Canaanite nation made a treaty contrary to the direction of God.

Solomon compared deceit to crockery covered in silver embellishments: "Fervent lips with a wicked heart are like earthenware covered with silver dross" (Prov. 26:23). This proverb is very similar to Jesus's comparison of the hypocrisy of the Pharisees to whitewashed tombs in Matthew 23:27. Whitewash on the outside of the tombs or silver decorations on the outside of the crockery does not disguise the rotting flesh in the tombs or deceit in the crockery. Deceit on our lips reflects the deceit in our hearts.

Wise Words

The proverbial woman used the best type of words: "She opens her mouth with wisdom, and on her tongue is the law of kindness" (Prov. 31:26). We all hope that such a legacy is ours! The proverbial woman had so many accomplishments. She was wealthy. She had wonderful children, servants, a vineyard, a thriving business, a husband who was a city leader, and a harmonious household. What she said while she achieved so much mattered as much as the accomplishments. People trusted this woman's words because she had a history of virtuous actions and wise words. Jesus's parable in Luke 16 is applicable for behavior as it is for money.

> *He who is faithful in what is least is faithful also in much, and he who is unjust in what is least is unjust also in much. Therefore if you have not been faithful in the unrighteous mammon, who will commit to your trust the true riches?* (Luke 16:10-11).

It is important to use wise words in small situations as well as big situations. We cannot measure the impact of our words on someone else. The proverbial woman was trusted by those with whom she associated. Why? Because her words and her actions were virtuous and noble. As a result, others will seek her counsel regarding their problems and dreams.

Maybe the first rule of wise words is not to speak rashly. "The heart of the righteous studies how to answer, but the mouth of the wicked pours forth evil" (Prov. 15:28). When we say the first thing that comes to mind, have we considered what the other person has said? Consider this diagram by Steven Covey about listening. Attentive and empathetic listening is required to understand what is being said by the other person and to have a wise response.

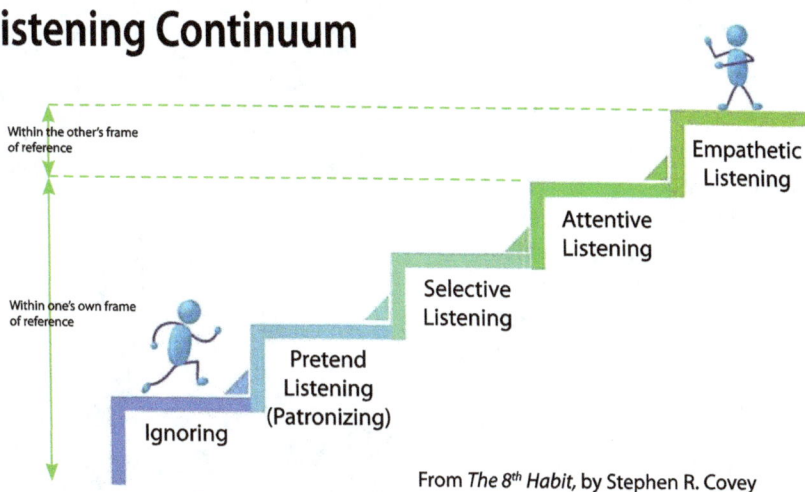

From *The 8th Habit*, by Stephen R. Covey

Another rule for wise words—wise words do not mean the highest quantity of words or the loudest words. "The tongue of the wise uses knowledge rightly, but the mouth of fools pours forth foolishness" (Prov. 15:2). The way that we say our wise words is as important as the words themselves.

Remember wise Abigail, who used quiet, gentle words to calm angry David and prevented David from seeking vengeance against Nabal (1 Sam. 25). Her husband's inebriated response to David's young men had been arrogant and mocking and poured forth the foolishness of Proverbs 15:2. Can you imagine drunken Nabal posturing in front of his household to prove his superiority to David?

Meanwhile, Abigail prepared provisions for David's men and set out on a donkey to personally deliver them. She was respectful, and her speech to David was not long nor loud. She spoke only to David, but all could see her actions. Wise Abigail saved the day and Nabal's household! A wise person does not have to talk the most or talk the loudest! Solomon summarized this situation perfectly: "Words of the wise, spoken quietly, should be heard rather than the shout of a ruler of fools. Wisdom is better than weapons of war" (Eccl. 9:17-18). Wonder if Solomon was thinking of Abigail when he penned that proverb?

The third rule for wise words is to use kind words anytime that we can: "Pleasant words are like a honeycomb, Sweetness to the soul, and health to the bones" (Prov. 16:24). In Bible times, honey was healthy food and was a sweetener. This proverb says that pleasant words are good for both your soul and your body and sweet to your ears. Spending time with others with pleasant words is good for anyone.

The elders gave this advice to King Rehoboam at the beginning of his reign: "If you are kind to these people, and please them, and speak good words to them, they will be your servants forever" (2 Chron. 10:6-8). Rehoboam rejected this advice and became a harsh king over the Israelite people. This harshness precipitated the revolt against Rehoboam. The elders were not advocating that Rehoboam be a push-over for the Israelites. They knew that a king required taxes and executed justice but were promoting kindness as the method for dealing with the people. Our words and actions matter!

The fourth rule for wise words is to speak those words at the right time. This rule implies there are right and wrong times for us to offer wise counsel.

A word spoken in due season, how good it is (Prov. 15:23b).

A word fitly spoken is like apples of gold in a setting of silver (Prov. 25:11).

It is always a good time to praise or compliment someone sincerely: "Therefore, as we have opportunity, let us do good to all, especially to those who are of the household of faith" (Gal. 6:10). These praises or compliments are not empty flattery, but truthful, honest statements to encourage the receiver. No one can make sincere comments without observation and involvement

Wise Words

with the other person. Wise words require knowledge and understanding of the receiver of those words.

It is always a good time to sow seed in the kingdom. However, one cannot expect to go from sowing seed to harvest in one conversation. Paul said, "I planted, Apollos watered, but God gave the increase" (1 Cor. 3:6). Wise words understand where the listener is in the harvest cycle and are different to someone who has never heard the gospel than someone who has heard years of lessons. It is always the right time to speak of the gospel, but our words must address the maturity of the listener's gospel knowledge. Remember, Paul said, "So then faith comes by hearing, and hearing by the word of God" (Rom. 10:17).

Picking the right time for wise words in other situations is hard. Considering how you would hear advice if you were in the listener's position might help but is not always applicable. It is easier to know the right time when you have a relationship with the other person, but that is not always the situation either.

The right time for wise words never comes if you are not an example of those wise words. "Be an example to the believers in word, in conduct, in love, in spirit, in faith, in purity" (1 Tim. 4:12b). To have wise words, we must walk our talk!

The last rule for wise words is sometimes silence speaks the loudest. Solomon wrote, "Even a fool is counted wise when he holds his peace: when he shuts his lips, he is considered perceptive" (Prov. 17:28). No one must respond to every word spoken to them. Jesus often responded to the Pharisees with silence. John 8:1-11 is a good example of Jesus's wise words of silence.

> They said to Him, "Teacher, this woman was caught in adultery, in the very act. Now Moses, in the law, commanded us that such should be stoned. But what do You say?" This they said, testing Him, that they might have something of which to accuse Him. But Jesus stooped down and wrote on the ground with His finger, as though He did not hear (vv. 4-6).

Jesus knew the Pharisees did not make their questions in good faith, and verbal sparring with them taught nothing. The Pharisees continued accusations and questioning brought a single statement from Jesus and then more silence. "He who is without sin among you, let him throw a stone at her first" (John 8:7b). Silence sometimes is the wisest of words!

Discussion Questions

1. When are we gossiping, and when are we relating facts to help a situation?

2. Did the Gibeonites/Hivites sin when they used deceiving words to fool the Israelites? Why or why not?

3. Why did Paul warn women about gossip and slander in 1 Timothy 3:11, 1 Timothy 5:13, and Titus 2:3?

4. Is today's "small talk," the same as "idle chatter" in Proverbs 14:23? In all labor, there is profit, but idle chatter leads only to poverty (Prov. 14:23). Why or why not?

5. How are praises and compliments different from empty flattery?

6. Explain Proverbs 26:20: "Where there is no wood, the fire goes out; and where there is no talebearer, strife ceases."

7. The lesson quotes 2 Timothy 3:2-5 related to slander. What other ways do these verses relate to our speech?

8. How can a sinful person offer wise words?

9. Can you suggest more "rules" for wise words?

Maturing in Body and Spirit

Lesson 11—Maturing in Body and Spirit

Charm is deceitful and beauty is passing (Prov. 31:30a).

The proverbial wife, so eloquently described in the last half of chapter 31, is not the only teaching in the chapter for the women of today. The beginning of the chapter features the words of King Lemuel's mother, and maybe, the last half of the chapter contain her words as well. She wanted her son to be a wise and just ruler who put the needs of the people above his own.

The words of King Lemuel, the utterance which his mother taught him: What, my son? And what, son of my womb? And what, son of my vows? Do not give your strength to women, Nor your ways to that which destroys kings. It is not for kings, O Lemuel, It is not for kings to drink wine, Nor for princes intoxicating drink; Lest they drink and forget the law, And pervert the justice of all afflicted. Give strong drink to him who is perishing, And wine to those who are bitter of heart. Let him drink and forget his poverty, And remember his misery no more. Open your mouth for the speechless, In the cause of all who are appointed to die. Open your mouth, judge righteously, And plead the cause of the poor and needy (vv. 1-9).

For this lesson, the point of the above verses is the source of the advice. King Lemuel should have heeded these words as they were from an older, wiser person who cared for him. If he was smart, he would have understood that an older person has had the opportunity to learn by living and more years to experience, study, observe, apply, and correct. Wisdom and understanding come with age for most people.

Does not the ear test words and the mouth taste its food? Wisdom is with aged men, and with length of days, understanding. With Him are wisdom and strength, He has counsel and understanding (Job 12:11-13).

Maturing in the Body

First, let me, the author, admit surprise at my age. I don't know when all those years went by, and I should still be twenty-something. The Lord has blessed me beyond words. I have good health, a wonderful husband and family, and a strong church congregation. Still, it is sobering to know that one has lived most of her years.

Maturing in the body is a natural process—our bodies age from young and strong to wrinkled and achy. God made us this way and did not mean for us to prefer our earthly bodies over His promised heavenly bodies. He wants our vision to be set on heaven as we live here on earth. Jesus said "Do not lay up for yourselves treasures on earth, where moth and rust destroy and where thieves break in and steal; but lay up for yourselves treasures in heaven, where neither moth nor rust destroys and where thieves do not break in and steal" (Matt. 6:19-20). Jesus is teaching us to prefer heavenly things over our earthly bodies and possessions.

The proverbial woman teaches us that *beauty is passing* as aging is natural (Prov. 31:30a). The beauty of our earthly bodies fades as we grow older. Our bodies grow from babies to young adults to gray-headed older people. During this process, some people are prettier and more handsome than others, and some are smarter, stronger, and quicker. All of us have different opportunities and abilities and will have achieved many different things as we age. However, just because we decide that we are old and that someone else has more resources or abilities than we do, does not mean God has decided that also. God expects all people to labor in His kingdom. Being older is not an exception.

All people can work in God's kingdom and have wonderful gifts to offer others along the way—both the older and younger workers in the kingdom. "Those who are planted in the house of the Lord shall flourish in the courts of our God. They shall still bear fruit in old age; they shall be fresh and flourishing, to declare that the Lord is upright; He is my rock, and there is no unrighteous-

Maturing in Body and Spirit

ness in Him" *(Ps. 92:13-15)*. We can retire from our jobs and careers, but we cannot retire from God. Reaching those golden years does not mean there is no work in our congregations and communities.

Paul teaches about special opportunities for mature Christians in Titus 2.

But as for you, speak the things which are proper for sound doctrine: that the older men be sober, reverent, temperate, sound in faith, in love, in patience; the older women likewise, that they be reverent in behavior, not slanderers, not given to much wine, teachers of good things—that they admonish the young women to love their husbands, to love their children, to be discreet, chaste, homemakers, good, obedient to their own husbands, that the word of God may not be blasphemed. Likewise, exhort the young men to be sober-minded, in all things showing yourself to be a pattern of good works; in doctrine showing integrity, reverence, incorruptibility, sound speech that cannot be condemned, that one who is an opponent may be ashamed, having nothing evil to say of you (vv. 1-8).

Older Christian men and women have many responsibilities in God's kingdom!

God wants the younger to respectfully learn from older people because all can learn from the past.

Honor your father and your mother, that your days may be long upon the land which the Lord your God is giving you (Exod. 20:12).

You shall rise before the gray-headed and honor the presence of an old man, and fear your God: I am the Lord (Lev. 19:32).

Though your beginning was small, Yet your latter end would increase abundantly. For inquire, please, of the former age, And consider the things discovered by their fathers; For we were born yesterday, and know nothing, Because our days on earth are a shadow (Job 8:7-9).

Do not rebuke an older man, but exhort him as a father, younger men as brothers, older women as mothers, younger women as sisters, with all purity (1 Tim. 5:1-2).

Maturing in the Spirit

Maturing in the spirit is growth in spiritual wisdom and practice. This growth is not entirely quantifiable as years measure age, but it is certainly visible. There are stages to this growth, similar to bodily growth. However, the stages of spiritual growth are not tied to years, as is bodily growth. Spiritual growth relates to our decisions. Each of us must decide and put in the work to grow closer to God. This work and closeness to God reflect our spiritual maturity and cause us to grow in our faith.

Body Growth	Spiritual Growth
Babe and youth	Building a spiritual foundation
Young adult	Growing in faith
Older adult	Teaching others

Building a Spiritual Foundation

At the time of one's baptism, no one knows everything about God and what God wants from her. God did NOT make that a requirement for salvation. He knows that each person can learn something new about Him and His word every day of their life. He does expect that we grow in our faith and our knowledge of Him.

> *But you, beloved, building yourselves up on your most holy faith, praying in the Holy Spirit, keep yourselves in the love of God, looking for the mercy of our Lord Jesus Christ unto eternal life* (Jude 20-21).

No one builds a house without first laying the foundation on which the whole of the house rests. Neither one can play a game without first knowing the rules. Our faith is not any different. If we have no plan to grow our faith and to know God's word, we will not build a spiritual foundation. We cannot believe in the Bible, if we don't know what it says and never open it. We cannot have faith in God if we do not know anything about Him. To know God, we must first have the desire to know Him.

> *Therefore, laying aside all malice, all deceit, hypocrisy, envy, and all evil speaking, as newborn babes, desire the pure milk of the word, that you may grow thereby, if indeed you have tasted that the Lord is gracious* (1 Pet. 2:1-3).

Many people say they believe in God and the Bible, but don't know anything about either. During the Sermon on the Mount, Jesus taught that real belief and faith in God must result in obedience to God. "Not everyone who says to Me, 'Lord, Lord,' shall enter the kingdom of heaven, but he who does the will of My Father in heaven" (Matt. 7:21). These people crying "Lord, Lord" have made no effort to know God or what He wants from them. They live on earth with no respect for God or fear of God. Being a moral person is not necessarily being a godly person.

Maturing in Body and Spirit

2 Peter 1 summarizes the strategy for building a spiritual foundation.

But also for this very reason, giving all diligence, add to your faith virtue, to virtue knowledge, to knowledge self-control, to self-control perseverance, to perseverance godliness, to godliness brotherly kindness, and to brotherly kindness love. For if these things are yours and abound, you will be neither barren nor unfruitful in the knowledge of our Lord Jesus Christ. For he who lacks these things is shortsighted, even to blindness, and has forgotten that he was cleansed from his old sins (2 Pet. 1:5-9).

These qualities all contribute to our spiritual foundation and growing in faith.

Growing in Faith

Growing in faith is an activity that a Christian must do throughout their life. Growing is an action verb, and action verbs define a process of doing something to achieve a goal. The verb "growing" means becoming greater or increasing over some time. A Christian's goal is to increase his or her faith and to live with God in heaven. A person's faith must increase over time to grow. Faith with a strong spiritual foundation is not static. It is constantly becoming deeper, more complex, richer, and stronger.

Faith with a strong foundation has diligence, virtue, knowledge, self-control, perseverance, godliness, brotherly kindness, and love. It takes a lifetime to address and grow all these qualities! A mature faith in God is more desirable than earthly beauty, wealth, and power. These earthly attributes are worthless after our death or God's judgment.

Diligence

In verse 5, Peter advises us to increase our faith "in all diligence." Diligence involves a persistent, hard-working effort to accomplish something. Peter knew time and energy were required to increase a person's faith. Christians require diligence to reach their goal of being with God in heaven. Growing in our faith and living with God does not happen without time and attention on our parts. A Christian's life is one of work.

Virtue

Some Bible translations may use the word "courage" here, and that may be a clearer meaning in today's vernacular. It was dangerous to be a Christian in the Roman world, and courage was necessary to be faithful in the gospel. However, danger does not only exist in the Roman arena. Today's Christian faces cultural and political danger. For example, to prove that you are not prejudiced, Christians are asked to embrace sexual practices forbidden in the Bible, and they are asked to approve of abortions to allow a woman control over her body. Virtue and courage are essential to growing faith!

Knowledge

Adding knowledge to faith requires dedicated continuation of Bible study. In Paul's letter to the Corinthians, he says, "Your faith should not be in the wisdom of men but in the power of God. However, we speak wisdom among those who are mature, yet not the wisdom of this age, nor of the rulers of this age, who are coming to nothing. But we speak the wisdom of God in a mystery, the hidden wisdom which God ordained before the ages for our glory" (1 Cor. 2:5-7). Christians must first seek to know and understand God before seeking earthly glories. A Christian must be mature in her faith and knowledge of God's word to properly discern and apply His word throughout her earthly life.

Self-control

Other synonyms for self-control are willpower, discipline, and restraint. Christians must master their passions rather than be controlled by them. Self-control can be as simple as not upbraiding a salesclerk for their mistake or seeking revenge for a fraudulent act. At the time of Peter's writing, false teachers (i.e., the Gnostics) preached that knowledge freed people from the need to control their passions. Today we have similar false ideas, such as the prosperity gospel. Our passions, not tempered in God's word, can lead us away from the Bible's gospel.

Perseverance

Perseverance is steady and continued action over a long period despite difficulties. Sometimes patience is translated here. Someone once told me that the key to perseverance is remembering our Father is in control of everything. When we know God is large and in charge, we can courageously persevere. My mom is the best example of this. As Amyotrophic Lateral Sclerosis (ALS) progressed throughout her body, her faith grew and shone as a light on the hill. Mom persevered; because her goal was heaven, not earth.

Godliness

Godliness involves actions that are well-pleasing to God. We cannot be well-pleasing to God in our actions if we do not demonstrate kindness to others. 1 John 4:20 captures this idea. "If someone says, 'I love God,' and hates his brother, he is a liar; for he who does not love his brother whom he has seen, how can he love God whom he has not seen?"

Remember Jesus's miracles? Jesus was kind to the most sinful of persons. He gently rebuked them and taught them about the gospel. He healed sinners, ate with sinners, and loved sinners. Godliness is treating others as Jesus would have treated them. This idea inspired the phrase "What would Jesus do?" in our popular culture.

However, godliness is not the same as tolerance. Godliness does not tolerate sin. Jesus told the adulterous woman, "Go and sin no more" (John 8:11). To be godly, this woman had to cease her sinful activities.

Brotherly kindness

The Greek word *philadelphia*, translated "brotherly kindness," signifies "the love of brothers." Christians are to consider the needs of others throughout their earthly lives. Brotherly kindness is a demonstration of God's kind of love. Many verses in the New Testament guide us in brotherly kindness.

> *Now as to the love of the brethren, you have no need for anyone to write to you, for you yourselves are taught by God to love one another* (1 Thess. 4:9).

> *Be devoted to one another in brotherly love; give preference to one another in honor* (Rom. 12:10).

> *Beloved, let us love one another, for love is from God; and everyone who loves is born of God and knows God. The one who does not love does not know God, for God is love. By this, the love of God was manifested in us, that God has sent His only begotten Son into the world so that we might live through Him* (1 John 4:7-9).

> *Owe nothing to anyone except to love one another; for he who loves his neighbor has fulfilled the law. For this, "you shall not commit adultery, you shall not murder, you shall not steal, you shall not covet, " and if there is any other commandment, it is summed up in this saying, "you shall love your neighbor as yourself." love does no wrong to a neighbor; therefore love is the fulfillment of the law* (Rom. 13:8-10).

One modern meme says, "You can always be kind," but God taught this idea first.

Maturing in Body and Spirit

Lesson 11

Love

The Greek word for this love is *agape* and is the highest type of love. It is more the kind of love God has for sinful, unworthy men. We are to love because we are from God. For example, in the book of John, Jesus commands us multiple times to love one another.

> *A new commandment I give to you, that you love one another; as I have loved you, that you also love one another. By this all will know that you are My disciples, if you have love for one another* (John 13:34-35).

> *This is My commandment that you love one another as I have loved you* (John 15:12).

> *These things I command you, that you love one another* (John 15:17).

Loving one another shows our obedience to God's commandments and our love for God.

> *By this, we know that we love the children of God, when we love God and keep His commandments* (1 John 5:2).

> *And this commandment we have from Him: that he who loves God must love his brother also* (1 John 4:21).

Teaching Others

We demonstrate Christian maturity when we teach others. Mature Christians must be ready to tell others about their faith in God and to teach others the gospel. Paul tells us this in his letter to Timothy: "Preach the word! Be ready in season and out of season. Convince, rebuke, exhort, with all longsuffering and teaching" (2 Tim. 4:1-2).

We are greedy and not Christ-like when we keep God's word to ourselves. How can we let someone be condemned to everlasting torment when we have the keys to His kingdom? Shout God's word from the mountaintops! Be counted as a soldier for Christ! A convicted Christian cannot have faith in the gospel without someone teaching him: "So then faith comes by hearing, and hearing by the word of God" (Rom. 10:17). Teach others about the gospel and your faith!

Lacking the courage to teach someone of the gospel is not a new problem. Christians of the first century had similar fears to ours. They were not sure they knew enough. They were not sure they knew what to say or how to say it. They were not different than we are today in this respect. The only difference is that they had the apostle Paul in their midst to be their encourager.

For though by this time you ought to be teachers, you need someone to teach you again the first principles of the oracles of God; and you have come to need milk and not solid food. For everyone who partakes only of milk is unskilled in the word of righteousness, for he is a babe. But solid food belongs to those who are of full age, that is, those who by reason of use have their senses exercised to discern both good and evil (Heb. 5:12-14).

Paul is our encourager, too. His words in Hebrews ring as loudly today as they did in the first century. He is speaking directly to each of us in the Hebrew letter and encouraging us to act our age and teach others about the gospel. Babies drink milk, need lots of care, and grow into adults. Adults eat meat and look after everyone in the family, both young and old. Adults consider the needs of the slaves, servants, and family members. Adults teach the knowledge and skills to survive to the young. Being an adult has responsibilities in a family. Being a mature Christian has similar responsibilities. God does not want us to hide the light of the gospel under a basket, but to let it shine from the hill.

Sometimes we are cautious about teaching others because we are afraid that we will not remember the appropriate verses or teach incorrectly. When you cannot remember the correct verse or an appropriate answer for a question, it is acceptable to say, "let me study and get back to you." As for teaching incorrectly, remember Apollos. He was an enthusiastic teacher of the gospel but only knew about John's baptism. Priscilla and Aquila took him aside and taught him the gospel more accurately. Apollos continued to be a vigorous gospel preacher (Acts 18:24-28). The best thing to remember is that Paul planted, Apollos watered, and God gave the increase (1 Cor. 3:6). All God asks is that we teach.

As we grow in spiritual maturity, we must decide between earthy and spiritual wisdom, as Paul said in Hebrews 5:14. We must "discern both good and evil." We must be able to tell the difference in God's way and the world's way. Often our culture presents sin as desirable and godly. To be wise "in this age" is to know all about current entertainment, political correctness, and tolerance to others' view of sin. Paul advises us to throw out worldly knowledge as it is foolish.

Let no one deceive himself. If anyone among you seems to be wise in this age, let him become a fool that he may become wise. For the wisdom of this world is foolishness with God. For it is written, "He catches the wise in their own craftiness" (1 Cor. 3:18-19).

Where is the wise? Where is the scribe? Where is the disputer of this age? Has not God made foolish the wisdom of this world? (1 Cor. 1:20).

Maturing in Body and Spirit

Conclusion

God wants all Christians, young and old, to work in His kingdom. There is no retirement plan while we are on earth! Throughout our earthly lives, all Christians can continue to grow in their faith. We will never learn all there is to know about God or His word.

Discussion Questions

1. Depending on your age, what can you teach a younger person, or what can you learn from an older person?

2. How and why might an older person look at God and heaven differently than a younger person?

3. Is there a time of life when you have nothing to teach or work to do?

4. Since "beauty is passing," is it sinful to work to maintain a youthful appearance as a person gets older?

5. Does 1 Timothy 5:1 teach that an older man cannot be corrected?

6. What is the difference between a moral person and a godly person?

7. How does faith become deeper, more complex, richer, and stronger?

8. First-century Christians often faced painful deaths for themselves and their families. Is it harder to be a Christian today than it was for 1st century Christians?

9. How is tolerance of sin versus godliness viewed in today's culture?

10. Some verses talk about love for our brethren, and some talk about love for others. What is the difference?

11. Often godliness, brotherly kindness, and love are taught in the same verse. How are these qualities the same? How are they different?

12. Must the qualities in 2 Peter 1:5-9 be obtained in the order listed? Why or why not?

13. What responsibilities does a mature Christian have for others?

14. What discernment must a Christian have related to?

    Scientific knowledge

    Social customs

    Religious freedom

    Other current issues

15. How can we teach others today?

The Storms of Life

Lesson 12—The Storms of Life

She also rises while it is yet night . . . She extends her hand to the poor, yes, she reaches out her hands to the needy . . . . She watches over the ways of her household and does not eat the bread of idleness (vv. 15a, 20, 27).

The verses in Proverbs 31 about the virtuous woman do not specifically call out the storms of her life. However, she watches over her household, looking for want and illness. She is mindful of her community, especially the poor and needy. No one's earthly existence is free of difficulties. This Biblical example had the same difficulties in her life as we have in our lives and experienced trials related to her general worries, marriage, family, community, nation, health, and security.

General Worries and Anxiety

Today, we live in an anxious society. Media describes the gory details of a house fire on the other side of our nation as if it happened next door and reports murder and abuse as if it happened in your city. I am not saying that house fires, murder, and abuse do not occur locally, as they certainly do. However, anxiety is created within an individual when worried about those faraway house fires, murder, and abuse. Sometimes our worry is about things that might happen, such as work layoffs or improbable events, such as national take-over

by space aliens. Continual apprehension about the evil in the world could cause doubts in our faith.

Remembering God's promise to be with each of us is the best way to fight anxiety and prevent those doubts. God knows that our lives can become difficult but wants His people to look to Him for strength. The following prayer from Psalm 119 shows us that being anxious is not a problem unique to us today.

> *My soul clings to the dust; Revive me according to Your word. I have declared my ways, and You answered me; Teach me Your statutes. Make me understand the way of Your precepts; So shall I meditate on Your wonderful works. My soul melts from heaviness; Strengthen me according to Your word. Remove from me the way of lying, And grant me Your law graciously. I have chosen the way of truth; Your judgments I have laid before me. I cling to Your testimonies; O Lord, do not put me to shame! I will run the course of Your commandments, For You shall enlarge my heart* (Ps. 119:25-32).

When we are worried and anxious, we are not alone—God is with us.

Marital Struggles

Everyone gets annoyed with her spouse. Anyone claiming to never have a cross word with her sweetheart is not telling the truth! However, annoyance can become a struggle which can become a marital problem. All couples must work on their marriage to prevent annoyance from becoming a serious issue in their marriage.

Biblical people had marital problems too. Job's wife advised him "to curse God and die" (Job 2:9). David's adultery with Bathsheba resulted in the murder of Uriah and the death of the child conceived during the affair.

The Storms of Life

Many things contribute to marital issues. Today we often hear these excuses.

Our culture actively promotes promiscuity.

- Role models are immoral and hold prominent positions within our society.
- Boredom with our spouse causes our thoughts and action to wander to another.
- Our spouse is unlovable.
- Money is tight.
- Children are insolent.
- The in-laws are intrusive.

Excuses abound for marital discord!

God meant for a marriage to be a haven from the onslaughts of the world. However, sometimes this is not the reality for a couple. Within a marriage, you can only control yourself and hope that your example influences your spouse. Some ideas for handling martial struggles are:

Treat Your Spouse Respectfully

God made marriage. He told us to leave all others and cling to our spouse (Gen. 2:24). God made us all in His image and loved His creation: "Nevertheless, neither is man independent of woman, nor woman independent of man, in the Lord. For as woman came from man, even so man also comes through woman; but all things are from God" (1 Cor. 11:11-12). We have different earthly roles; however, God wants us to treat our spouses respectfully and to treat them as we want to be treated.

Live Within Your Means

Don't spend more than you make, and always save something for a rainy day (Isa. 55:2).

Resist Modern Morals and Cling to God's Commandments

Do you not know that the unrighteous will not inherit the kingdom of God? Do not be deceived. Neither fornicators, nor idolaters, nor adulterers, nor homosexuals, nor sodomites, nor thieves, nor covetous, nor drunkards, nor revilers, nor extortioners will inherit the kingdom of God. And such were some of you. But you were washed, but you were sanctified, but you were justified in the name of the Lord Jesus and by the Spirit of our God (1 Cor. 6:9-11).

Avoid Tempting Situations and Flee If Necessary

Tempting situations can include overspending, sex, alcohol, or any number of circumstances. Joseph was a slave tasked with the management of Potiphar's estate. Joseph fled from Potiphar's wife, who desired sex with Joseph, even though he knew that it would result in punishment. Be like Joseph and obey God!

Teach Your Children

Parents are not responsible for the sins of grown children (Ezek. 18:20). However, a parent is to teach his or her children about God (Deut. 6:6-9). Our children cannot know how God helps us each day if we don't tell them.

When our marriage is struggling, we are not alone as God is with us.

Family Issues

No family is perfect. For example, Adam and Eve's son, Cain, killed his brother. Jacob and Rebekah schemed to steal Esau's blessing. Laban tricked Jacob into marrying Leah. Samuel's and Eli's sons did not follow God. Absalom rebelled and tried to steal his father, David's crown. Family issues have happened as long as there have been families.

Family issues can be hidden deep within the family. Secrecy hides physical and sexual abuse from those outside the family unit, and maybe, hides the abuse from members within the family unit. Secrecy hides adultery, overspending, theft, cheating, and all sorts of family secrets. Older, stronger family members take advantage of younger and weaker members. Members of a family do not always live by the golden rule: "And just as you want men to do to you, you also do to them likewise" (Luke 6:31).

At other times, one or both parents are absent from the family unit. This absence may be due to job requirements, military deployment, death, divorce, incarceration, or drug/alcohol addiction. Maybe the father doesn't know there is a child. Any of these and many other reasons leave an incomplete family unit.

The Storms of Life

There are too many family issues and too many applicable Scriptures to list them in this lesson. Each situation cries for a Biblical solution. However, God made the family unit and wanted that unit to be righteous. Ephesians 5 has a lot to teach us about families and how to act toward members of the family. These verses tell us to:

Walk in Love

Therefore be imitators of God as dear children. And walk in love, as Christ also has loved us and given Himself for us, an offering and a sacrifice to God for a sweet-smelling aroma (Eph. 5:1-2).

Walk as Children of Light

For you were once darkness, but now you are light in the Lord. Walk as children of light (for the fruit of the Spirit is in all goodness, righteousness, and truth), finding out what is acceptable to the Lord (Eph. 5:8-10).

Walk Not as Fools but As Someone Who Knows God

See then that you walk circumspectly, not as fools but as wise, redeeming the time, because the days are evil. Therefore do not be unwise, but understand what the will of the Lord is (Eph. 5:15-17).

Walk as a Godly Member Within the Family Unit

Nevertheless let each one of you in particular so love his own wife as himself, and let the wife see that she respects her husband (Eph. 5:33).

When our families are stressed, we are not alone, as God is with us.

Community Problems

Community problems can also affect our relationship with God. Contentious discussions at a council meeting related to taxes, schools, roads, and development are common today. Hot tempers allow words to be cutting and ugly. Neighbors become suspicious of neighbors. Leadership is nullified and questioned. Often, we question or ignore God when our neighborhoods are not as we wish.

Korah's rebellion is an example. His neighborhood was the Israelite tribe (Num. 16:1-50). Korah was unhappy with his responsibilities as a Levite and wanted a position and prestige like Aaron's. He involved others in his disgruntlement leading to the destruction of hundreds of people. The aftermath of

TODAY'S VIRTUOUS WOMAN

God's judgment of Korah and his followers caused more complaining among the Israelites. Then God sent a plague to discipline the Israelites for their whispering. Yes, community problems can become our problems!

A Christian must act righteously even when the community does not. At times, we may feel that we are the only righteous individuals in our neighborhood. Elijah certainly knew that feeling! After escaping from Jezebel (1 Kings 19), Elijah declared to God that he was the only righteous person left. God told Elijah to get to work and that there are 7000 in Israel who had not bowed to Baal. God wants His people to act righteously within their community and to work in His kingdom.

When our communities are in turmoil, we are not alone, as God is with us.

National and Worldwide Matters

Often the world seems to be a merciless place full of hatred, poverty, disasters, murder, and many other aspects of evil. It can seem that one person cannot stand up under the weight of the world's problems. It is hard for a Christian to be faithful in these circumstances.

A cruel world is not a new thing. The world has been a hard place since Adam and Eve left the Garden of Eden. Think about living as a Christian under

The Storms of Life

Roman rule, especially if you actively preached and taught the gospel. Torture and death were often the result of Christians under the Romans. The apostle Paul was persecuted for his faith by both the Jewish leaders and the Romans. The following are just a few examples of his tribulations for preaching the gospel and declaring Jesus was Christ.

- He escaped attempted murder by Hellenists in Jerusalem (Acts 9:29).
- He was expelled from Antioch (Acts 13:50).
- He escaped stoning in Iconium (Acts 14:5-6).
- He was stoned and left for dead in Derbe (Acts 14:19).
- He was beaten and imprisoned with Silas in Philippi (Acts 22-23).
- The home where he was staying was attacked (Acts 17:5).
- The Jewish plotted against him in Greece (Acts 20:3).
- He was arrested in the temple (Acts 21:30, 33).
- He was imprisoned several times for several years in various Roman facilities.

It is helpful to remember that God put certain governments in charge for a reason as He did with Assyria and Babylon. This remembrance of God's power assures us that God knows what is happening today. When the world is cruel and unrighteous, we must be like Paul and declare Jesus regardless of the worldly consequences.

When the world is breaking, we are not alone as God is with us.

Health Battles

Good health is unappreciated until you don't have it anymore. Some of us have never enjoyed good health.

Possibly during Sennacherib's attack of Jerusalem, King Hezekiah became deathly sick (2 Kings 18:35-20:6). Hezekiah wept as he knew the nation of Judah needed his faith in God to defeat Assyria and prayed to God for help. God heard his prayers, added fifteen years to Hezekiah's life, and destroyed the Assyrian army. God's sign to Hezekiah of healing was to move the sundial backward ten degrees!

The apostle Paul tells us that he pleaded three times for his "thorn in the flesh" to be removed. However, God chose not to answer this prayer, causing Paul to lean more on God because of this infirmity. Paul said, "Therefore I take pleasure in infirmities, in reproaches, in needs, in persecutions, in distresses, for Christ's sake. For when I am weak, then I am strong" (2 Cor. 12:7-10).

God healed Hezekiah, but not Paul. Whether God gives us healing or not, our joy in God must remain steadfast. Joy is the theme of the book of Philippians. Paul writes about his gratitude toward the Philippians and his joy in God while he is in prison. Let God work through us during our health battles as He worked through Hezekiah and Paul. Others can see God in our lives and our joy in Him during our most difficult times.

When our health is failing, we are not alone as God is with us.

Security Concerns

Often, we are anxious when circumstances jeopardize our well-being. Financial crises, aging, and physical security are frequent concerns. These worries afflicted Biblical people too.

- The widow in 2 Kings 4:1 was facing a financial crisis so great that her two sons were being sold into slavery and begged the prophet, Elisha, for help.
- The widow of Nain's only son had died. A crowd was carrying the son's dead body out for burial. His mother faced poverty for the rest of her life (Luke 7:11-12).
- Rahab and the whole city of Jericho feared conquest by the Israelite army (Josh. 2:8-11). They were terrified of the Israelites and their God.

Good times and bad times have always happened. Paul reminds us that our citizenship is in heaven and comforts us with these words.

For our citizenship is in heaven, from which we also eagerly wait for the Savior, the Lord Jesus Christ, who will transform our lowly body that it may be conformed to His glorious body, according to the working by which He is able even to subdue all things to Himself (Phil. 3:20-21).

During His Sermon on the Mount, Jesus said, "Do not lay up for yourselves treasures on earth, where moth and rust destroy and where thieves break in and steal; but lay up for yourselves treasures in heaven, where neither moth nor rust destroys and where thieves do not break in and steal" (Matt. 6:19-20). Our security and well-being reside in heaven, not here on earth. It is nice to have those comforts while we live on earth. However, our goal is heaven, where our treasure is everlasting.

When we are afraid, we are not alone as God is with us.

The Storms of Life

Church Issues

The church represents Christ's body here on earth. Christians, as members of the body, are to love and support each other. Paul writes, "And let us consider one another in order to stir up love and good works, not forsaking the assembling of ourselves together, as is the manner of some, but exhorting one another, and so much the more as you see the Day approaching" (Heb. 10:24-25).

Weak or failing leadership causes distress in a church. Dissension among members causes division. Rumors and secrecy cause uncertainty and discouragement among weaker members. Family quarrels, personality clashes, and different offenses cause church members to take sides.

Unity among the church is God's goal. Paul pleads with the quarreling Corinthians, "Now I plead with you, brethren, by the name of our Lord Jesus Christ, that you all speak the same thing, and that there be no divisions among you, but that you be perfectly joined together in the same mind and in the same judgment" (1 Cor. 1:10). Unity must be our goal, too. All Christians must work on the problems within their assembly with patience, tolerance, and love.

A Christian must be certain that their faith is in God and not a person. Remember, we must follow Jesus, not merely a preacher or an elder. Paul warns us about basing our faith on an individual:

> Now I say this, that each of you says, "I am of Paul," or "I am of Apollos," or "I am of Cephas," or "I am of Christ." Is Christ divided? Was Paul crucified for you? Or were you baptized in the name of Paul? (1 Cor. 1:12–13).

> For the message of the cross is foolishness to those who are perishing, but to us who are being saved it is the power of God (1 Cor. 1:18).

Christian must study the Bible for themselves to be certain that they know the truth: "Therefore, my beloved, as you have always obeyed, not as in my presence only, but now much more in my absence, work out your own salvation with fear and trembling" (Phil. 2:12). Confidence in your faith and knowledge of God's word helps anyone stand upright when the local congregation is struggling.

Do not tolerate brother who will not repent. In his letter to the Romans, Paul advises, "Now I urge you, brethren, note those who cause divisions and offenses, contrary to the doctrine which you learned, and avoid them" (Rom. 16:17). The church of Thyatira was chastised for tolerating a sinning woman as her example caused others to sin. However, Paul also tells us that we are to be gentle with repentant brothers and sisters. "You ought rather to forgive and comfort him, lest perhaps such a one be swallowed up with too much sorrow" (2 Cor. 2:7b). We must forgive our repentant brothers as God has forgiven them already.

When our congregation has troubles, we are not alone as God is with us.

Prayer and Bible Reading

During all the storms of our lives, we are not alone as God is with us. He is there to strengthen and encourage us all the time. We must spend time with God in prayer and by reading His word.

People often say, "God does not ask more than we can do," which is not true. We often face huge trials, and God wants us to depend on Him to persevere. When more is required from us than we can do, God wants us to remember to lean on Him (1 Cor. 10:13). He did not intend for us to face life alone. This simple poem illustrates this idea.

Footprints in the Sand

One night I dreamed a dream.
As I was walking along the beach with my Lord.
Across the dark sky flashed scenes from my life.
For each scene, I noticed two sets of footprints in the sand,
One belonging to me and one to my Lord.

After the last scene of my life flashed before me,
I looked back at the footprints in the sand.
I noticed that, at many times along the path of my life,
especially at the very lowest and saddest times,
there was only one set of footprints.

The Storms of Life

> This really troubled me, so I asked the Lord about it.
> "Lord, you said once I decided to follow you,
> You'd walk with me all the way.
> But I noticed that during the saddest and most troublesome times of my life, there was only one set of footprints.
> I don't understand why, when I needed You the most, You would leave me."
>
> He whispered, "My precious child, I love you and will never leave you
> Never, ever, during your trials and testings.
> When you saw only one set of footprints,
> It was then that I carried you."

We are never alone as God is with us.

Discussion Questions

1. Can we express our worries and anxieties to God in prayer when we do not understand them ourselves?

2. How can our martial struggle affect our relationship with God?

3. What should we do when someone tells us of physical or sexual abuse by a family member?

4. Our communities are often racially divided. How can a Christian help?

5. How can a Christian influence state and national governments from unrighteous legislation?

6. Chronic disease and disability affect more than the afflicted person.

7. How can we support someone severely afflicted?

8. How can we support others if we are the afflicted person?

9. What advice would you give to someone anxious about their well-being?

10. For those who have experienced division within their assembly, what advice would you give to others?

11. The author recommends prayer and Bible reading during life's storms. What would be your advice?

12. What are your favorite Scriptures when you are troubled?

Who Fears the Lord

Lesson 13—Who Fears the Lord

Charm is deceitful and beauty is passing, But a woman who fears the Lord, she shall be praised (Prov. 31:30).

Fear of the Lord is awe and reverence for the majesty of God and confidence in Him to keep all His promises. This fear, coupled with deep humility from the person toward God, causes the person to strive for obedience to all of God's commandments and to be a righteous person both inside and out. The Proverbial woman's fear of the Lord is her most desirable quality and the one to be most admired.

Proverbs 31:10-31 is read at many funerals as we mourn the passing of our beloved wives, mothers, sisters, and friends. "A woman who fears the Lord" is the highest compliment of a well-lived life, and all of us desire to be known as a godly Proverbial woman. The book of James is a practical "how to" book for living a Christian life and gives wonderful guidance to help us reach our goal of

a righteous life on earth and an eternal life in heaven. This book explains how a righteous woman demonstrates their fear and honor of God. Let's consider a few ideas from James.

Purpose of Earthly Trials

James tells us that Christians can grow and thrive during their trails on earth. He encourages us to find the joy in our circumstances as the trouble and difficulties on earth test our faith:

> *My brethren, count it all joy when you fall into various trials, knowing that the testing of your faith produces patience. But let patience have its perfect work, that you may be perfect and complete, lacking nothing. If any of you lacks wisdom, let him ask of God, who gives to all liberally and without reproach, and it will be given to him* (Jas. 1:2-5).

The testing of our faith is not a pass/fail situation like a school test, but a growing/maturing process. "Test" is from the Greek word referring to the testing of gold coins to prove they were genuine. So, the testing of our faith is not to destroy or debase it, but to purge and refine it. Tests produce patience in us so that we can stand strong under worldly pressures, find our joy, and look for opportunities to spread the gospel.

> *Blessed is the man who endures temptation; for when he has been approved, he will receive the crown of life which the Lord has promised to those who love Him* (Jas. 1:12).

Loving God during our trials on earth can be hard as daily we are tempted by our desires. We can envy someone's house, feel bitterness for our coworker's promotion, become jealous of our friend's talents, desire more money, hate our social standing, feel spite for another's success, begrudge our offering at church, resent time spent with brethren, covet earthly success, or rail against our poor health. There is an abundance of earthly advice for any situation in which we find ourselves. Not all earthly advisors have godly advice! We show our love for God by our obedience to His commandments. Jesus told us, "If you love Me, keep My commandments" (John 14:15).

During our trials, our faith that God keeps all His promises must endure and grow. Endurance and growth are essential for all of us who will appear before the throne of God. "For we must all appear before the judgment seat of Christ, that each one may receive the things done in the body, according to what he has done, whether good or bad" (2 Cor. 5:10). Trials test our faith resulting in patience and endurance so that we can obtain God's promised crown.

Who Fears the Lord

Lesson 13

James has concise advice for the necessary qualities for enduring our trials. "So then, my beloved brethren, let every man be swift to hear, slow to speak, slow to wrath; for the wrath of man does not produce the righteousness of God" (Jas. 1:19-20). This guidance is stating that all Christians will have hard times and face temptation. James did not want to discourage the brethren, but to help them become stronger followers of God. Not only did James have this advice, but he tells us more about applying his guidance to our lives in the rest of his epistle.

Swift to Hear

One of the first verses that come to my mind about hearing the gospel is Romans 10:17. Paul writes, "So then faith comes by hearing, and hearing by the word of God." No one can know the gospel without first hearing it. We must tell others about the gospel so that all can have faith in God. However, a Christian's actions in their daily life affect how another person "hears" the gospel.

> But be doers of the word, and not hearers only, deceiving yourselves. For if anyone is a hearer of the word and not a doer, he is like a man observing his natural face in a mirror; for he observes himself, goes away, and immediately forgets what kind of man he was. But he who looks into the perfect law of liberty and continues in it, and is not a forgetful hearer but a doer of the work, this one will be blessed in what he does (Jas. 1:22-25).

If we truly believe the gospel and that God has a crown waiting for us, then our actions speak louder than our words. People of the world can "hear" our actions. James stresses that all Christians must be doers of the word to all the world so that the world can see our faith by our works. In Proverbs 23:26, Solomon wrote, "My son, give me your heart, and let your eyes observe my ways." Again, our actions speak louder than our words.

TODAY'S VIRTUOUS WOMAN

Dorcas was simply a woman in New Testament times. However, her charity in providing clothes to others was well-known in her community. During those days, most people only had one set of clothing, and a closet for clothes was not necessary. Dorcas's charity took a lot of her time and money. She was an outstanding example of a doer of the work (Jas. 1:25). She put her faith into action. Think of how many people would "hear" Dorcas's words about her faith in God.

Hearing is also affected by how a Christian treats other people. Do we act without partiality, and demonstrate God's love for all? "For God so loved the world that He gave His only begotten Son" (John 3:16). God loves all people. He wants all to be saved. Jesus died for all the people in the world so they could be saved. Shouldn't Christians love the people of the world as God and Jesus do? James teaches that we Christians cannot show favoritism by teaching some people and not others.

> *My brethren, do not hold the faith of our Lord Jesus Christ, the Lord of glory, with partiality . . . If you really fulfill the royal law according to the Scripture, "You shall love your neighbor as yourself," you do well; but if you show partiality, you commit sin* (Jas. 2:1, 8-9).

The royal law is stated in Leviticus 19:18, which says, "You shall not take vengeance, nor bear any grudge against the children of your people, but you shall love your neighbor as yourself: I am the Lord." In the parable of the good Samaritan, Jesus teaches us that the royal law requires active goodwill without partiality. The Samaritan helped a man who hated him when "spiritual" people had passed by the man (Luke 10:25-37).

The Levite and the priest were showing partiality against the beaten man and did not involve themselves with his situation. The love of God was not evident in their concern for him at all. They did not walk their talk about the royal law, so why would anyone listen to their spiritual message? James tells Christians to fulfill the royal law without partiality. Without partiality means without regard to social status, nationality, or bank accounts. God loves all the people and wants all the people to hear His gospel.

To Christians who don't realize that their works demonstrate their faith, James says, "For as the body without the spirit is dead, so faith without works is dead also" (Jas. 2:26). The world sees our faith by our works—that is how they "hear" our faith. James says, "If a brother or sister is naked and destitute of daily food, and one of you says to them, 'Depart in peace, be warmed and filled,' but you do not give them the things which are needed for the body, what does it profit? Thus also faith by itself, if it does not have works, is dead" (Jas. 2: 15-17). He is stressing to Christians that genuine faith is demonstrated to the world by actions.

For example, my husband met this senior lady several years ago. She heard and obeyed the gospel as a grown woman. She had *heard the word* from someone. She then taught all her immediate family, extended family, and community. This person was *swift to hear,* and with her works taught the gospel to so many people!

This lady would have been like Priscilla and Aquila. Priscilla and Aquila were tentmakers. However, they lived for the gospel as part of their everyday life. Their actions spoke to people and said they were different. Their words spoke to people as they told those people how to be different. People cannot be *swift to hear* if no one is speaking to them about the gospel!

Slow to Speak

In the section above, the discussion centered on our actions, but our words matter just as much. Our words tell the world a lot about our faith. James uses all of chapter 3 to remind Christians of this fact. James compares our tongues to a little fire that causes an inferno. "Even so the tongue is a little member and boasts great things. See how great a forest a little fire kindles! And the tongue is a fire, a world of iniquity" (Jas. 3:5-6a). The words we speak matter!

> Out of the same mouth proceed blessing and cursing. My brethren, these things ought not to be so. Does a spring send forth fresh water and bitter from the same opening? Can a fig tree, my brethren, bear olives, or a grapevine bear figs? Thus no spring yields both salt water and fresh (Jas. 3:10-12).

When a faithful people uses their mouths to both bless and curse, the world sees the contradiction and is not likely to *hear* their words of faith. After all, how can those words about the gospel be meaningful to the speakers, when curse words are just as likely to be spoken by them? These speakers have nullified any influence they might have over their listener who won't hear words about the gospel from this person!

James's advice is to be "slow to speak." Just as a bit controls a horse or a rudder controls a ship (Jas. 3:3-4), we must control our speech. Consider your words and stop the unrighteous ones! Heavenly wisdom is necessary to guide our speech.

> But the wisdom that is from above is first pure, then peaceable, gentle, willing to yield, full of mercy and good fruits, without partiality and without hypocrisy. Now the fruit of righteousness is sown in peace by those who make peace (Jas. 3:17-18).

Slow to Wrath

First, let us distinguish between divine wrath and human wrath. God's wrath is the natural expression of the divine nature, which is absolute holiness, manifesting itself against the willful, high-handed, deliberate, inexcusable sin and iniquity of mankind. Human wrath is the exhibition of an enraged sinful nature. Anger or righteous indignation is not the same as wrath. Anger itself is not sinful but can grow into sinful wrath.

Some examples of righteous anger were Jesus cleansing the temple (Mark 11:15), His anger at the hardness of the Pharisees' hearts (Mark 3:5), Moses at Pharaoh (Exod. 11:8), and Jacob when Laban chased him (Gen. 31:36). Some examples of unrighteous anger are Cain killing Abel (Gen. 4:5, 6), Moses's anger at the Israelites (Num. 20:10, 11), and the high priest jailing the apostles (Acts 5:17).

Some New Testament commandments about anger and wrath are:

> Be angry, and do not sin: do not let the sun go down on your wrath, nor give place to the devil (Eph. 4:26-27).

> But I say to you that whoever is angry with his brother without a cause shall be in danger of the judgment (Matt. 5:22).

> Beloved, do not avenge yourselves, but rather give place to wrath; for it is written, "Vengeance is Mine, I will repay, " says the Lord. Therefore "If your enemy is hungry, feed him; If he is thirsty, give him a drink; For in so doing you will heap coals of fire on his head" (Rom. 12:19-20).

> And you, fathers, do not provoke your children to wrath, but bring them up in the training and admonition of the Lord (Eph. 6:4).

> Husbands, love your wives and do not be bitter toward them (Col. 3:19).

Who Fears the Lord

James's epistle has advice to Christians for managing their wrath. The first is, "Therefore submit to God. Resist the devil and he will flee from you. Draw near to God and He will draw near to you" (Jas. 4:7-8) Of course, submitting to God is the first step to any form of righteousness. A Christian must recognize that God's way is the only way to achieve the prize of eternal life with God. To do this, we are giving up earthly ideals and priorities. When we have our eyes on the prize, we can recognize when we are angry at sin or have sinful anger and wrath. This realization causes us to resist the devil who must flee from someone in the army of God. James assures us that God draws near and is with us when we seek Him. Humility and forsaking human pride are qualities that help Christians to obey God's commandments against unrighteous anger and wrath. "Humble yourselves in the sight of the Lord, and He will lift you up" (Jas. 4:10).

James's second piece of advice is against judging brethren against the law of Christ. "Do not speak evil of one another, brethren. He who speaks evil of a brother and judges his brother, speaks evil of the law and judges the law. But if you judge the law, you are not a doer of the law but a judge" (Jas. 4:11) The point here is that a Christian should not have a spirit of criticism and fault-finding. Yes, Christians must often judge, as in, evaluating a person or situation for righteousness before participating in an activity or endeavor. Exercising righteous judgment is necessary to obey God's commandments. However, as we judge, we must remember that God is the ultimate judge over His law, and He will be the final judge of everyone (Jas. 4:12).

Thirdly, James reminds us that we should not be arrogant with our earthly successes because we need God in our lives. We should say, "If the Lord wills, we shall live and do this or that." James rebuked the disciples, saying, "But now you boast in your arrogance. All such boasting is evil" (Jas. 4:15-16). Self-reliance is a valued character trait, and God does want us to work. However, when self-reliance moves God out of the way, it is sinful. Planning, hard work, and self-reliance are not necessarily sinful. The sin is leaving God out of the planning and hard work. An arrogant person believes that all an individual has accomplished was a personal achievement, forgetting that God is over everything.

Jesus's parable about the rich fool in Luke 12:16-20 teaches about earthly arrogance. The rich fool had a great crop. He was planning to store all his abundance while relaxing and basking in his success. God required his soul that very night. The rich fool had forgotten God and was arrogant in his earthly success.

James's fourth point is to be patient for the coming of the Lord: "Therefore be patient, brethren, until the coming of the Lord. See how the farmer waits for the precious fruit of the earth, waiting patiently for it until it receives the early and latter rain. You also be patient. Establish your hearts, for the coming of the Lord is at hand" (Jas. 5:7-8). The context tells Christians to wait for the Lord during all their trials on earth, even when others treat them cruelly. We can let cruel treatment or trials to cause wrath, but patience helps us to prevent wrath. We do not know exactly when the Lord is coming, but James assures us the Jesus is coming again. Remember patience!

James's counsel related to humility, judging, arrogance, and patience all helps a Christian to manage her anger and to be "slow to wrath." He wants us to act in the manner that God is commanding us to act.

Helping Others to Return to God

Both James and the Proverbial woman had concern for others. Proverbs 31 has many verses describing the Proverbial woman's care of her family, household, and community. Sometimes her care may have included a backslider. The last verses of James 5 command us to care for the backsliders. "Brethren, if anyone among you wanders from the truth, and someone turns him back, let him know that he who turns a sinner from the error of his way will save a soul from death and cover a multitude of sins" (Jas. 5:19-20).

Who Fears the Lord

Helping a backslider to return to the fold of God is the most substantial evidence of the "fear of the Lord." The faithful Christian has saved the erring Christian from death! This work demonstrates the awe, reverence, and confidence that both persons have in God. Remember, God loves all the people of the world and wants all to be saved. Jesus died for all the people in the world so they could be saved. All the people of the world include the backsliders!

Conclusion

Often the highest compliment to a Christian is to acknowledge his or her "fear of the Lord." The book of James has practical guidance for Christians to fear the Lord and tells us to be swift to hear, be slow to speak, and be slow to wrath. His counsel includes that we show our faith by our good works, we cannot show partiality, we must control our tongue, we must think before we speak, we must be humble, we are not the final judge, we must rely on God, we must be patient, and we must return sinners to the fold.

Discussion Questions

1. How do we show fear of the Lord? Why does the fear of the Lord cause obedience? Is this desirable?

2. Why is it hard to find joy in our trials on earth?

3. In 2 Corinthians 5:10, is Paul warning us that our good or bad deeds are the determining factors in obtaining our crowns? Why or why not?

4. Why is Dorcas used as an example for "swift to hear'?

5. Can we help a brother or sister too much?

6. How can heavenly wisdom guide your speech?

7. How can we be known as someone who makes peace?

8. How can we know when we have feelings of righteous anger or sinful wrath?

9. What guidelines do you use to practice righteous judgment? How does judging lead to wrath?

10. What does arrogance have to do with wrath (as in slow to wrath)?

11. How is patience required to wait on the coming of Jesus?

12. How does helping a backslider demonstrate a person's fear of the Lord?

Sources

Coffman, James Burton. *Proverbs*. Abilene, TX: Abilene Christian University Press, 1974.

_____. *Judges and Ruth*. Abilene, TX: Abilene Christian University Press, 1974.

Covey, Stephen R. *The 8th Habit: From Effectiveness to Greatness*. New York: Free Press, 2004.

"Footprints in the Sand." The authorship of this poem is disputed. Three authors have claimed to have written it: Mary Stevensen (1936); Carolyn Carty (1963), and Margaret Fishback Powers (1964). The version used in this book does not match the versions attributed to any of these authors (see "Footprints in the Sand: An Amazing Poem in Search of Its Author." *Wowzone.com* [online] http://www.wowzone.com/fprints.htm. For an analysis of the origins and influences of the poem, see: "Footprints (poem)." *Wikipedia* [online] https://en.wikipedia.org/wiki/Footprints_(poem).

"Home." *Wikipedia* [online] https://en.wikipedia.org/wiki/Home.

Seeger, Pete. "Tutn, Turn, Trun." *A Traditional Music Library* [online] www.traditionalmusic.co.uk.

All images: istockphoto.com

www.ingramcontent.com/pod-product-compliance
Lightning Source LLC
LaVergne TN
LVHW021601070426
835507LV00015B/1897